Contents

Foreword

I have had the great honour and pleasure to travel a lot of the world for over a decade talking, advising and consulting about ICT and learning. It is a personal passion and, being married to a teacher, an issue that concerns me both professionally and personally. When I started I met many enthusiasts who shared a dream that we could use ICT to transform the experience of education and deliver a global aspiration of education for every citizen of the world. Against these lofty ambitions the perennial constraints of budgets, political will and professional inertia were easily visible. There were many fears expressed to me. Most importantly, there was a concern that, somehow, ICT would be used as an excuse to sack teachers and close schools and pump learning into kids' heads through impersonal technology.

Being an optimist, my experience over the last decade has kept those lofty aspirations alive. It has also made the fundamental truths about both education and learning clear to me. First, learning is at its heart a social and a socializing experience. ICTs are very powerful tools, but smart technologies need smart people, they don't replace them. In a world where technology is increasingly pervasive, teachers become more not less important.

Second, as the world becomes increasingly connected, as technology and science develop at an ever increasing pace, the economic and social future of any country is increasingly tied to its commitment to education and training, not just for the elite but for every citizen and community.

Third, the goal is not just raising standards but changing culture. I describe this using the analogy of the driving test, a rite of passage for many young people. The emerging global information society requires us to create a new generation who, when they leave school, put on their L-plates and think 'I am a learner', rather than take them off and say 'I have passed'.

We can only make this happen on the scale needed if we value and invest in our teachers as lifelong learners themselves, not just in their 'subject skills'. To do this we need to marry the big picture of a transformed experience of learning to ICT practice, but also to new theories of learning such as learning styles or multiple intelligences. For teachers to be seen as learners themselves we need to build bridges between different areas of research – in education, learning theories, ICT and management, to name but a few.

Reading the first few titles in this series, it is wonderful to see words like creativity, personalization and exciting being based on actual evidence, not just lofty aspiration. The rate of change of technology in the next decade will at least match the progress in the last. The materials available to enrich good teaching and learning practice will grow exponentially. None of this will have the profound change that many aspire to if we cannot build the bridge between theory and what happens in individual lessons, be they in art, maths, music, history, modern languages or any other area of the curriculum.

The notion of ICT as a tool across the curriculum was greeted sceptically a decade ago. Many professionals told me that ICT may be important in maths or science, but irrelevant in the arts and humanities. My own experience is that the most exciting innovations have actually been in arts and humanities, while the notion of maths as a visual discipline seemed alien a few years ago. It has not been ICT but innovative teachers, researchers and indeed publishers who have pushed the art of the possible.

In a lot of my work, I have encouraged the notion that we should see the era we live in as a New Renaissance, rather than a new Industrial Revolution. While the industrial revolutions were about simplification and analysis, the era we live in is about synthesis and connection. We need our learners to embrace both depth and breadth to meet their needs to learn for life and living.

To the authors of this series, I offer my congratulations and sincere thanks. In bringing together the evidence of what works, the digital resources available and the new theories of learning, along with the new capabilities of ICT, they bring the focus onto the most important element of the transformation of learning, which to me is the learning needs of the teaching profession.

To the readers of this series, I make what I believe is my boldest claim. This is the greatest time in human history to be a teacher. Our societies and economies demand education like never before. Our increasing knowledge of how we learn and how the brain works, together with the availability of powerful ICT tools, make this a time when the creativity, professionalism and aspirations for a learning society are at a premium. Teaching is a noble profession. It is after all the profession that creates all the others.

There are many things that we do not yet know, so much to learn. That is what makes this so exciting. I and my colleagues at Microsoft can build the tools, but we believe that it is putting those tools in the hands of innovative, skilled and inspirational teachers that creates the real value.

I hope that after reading any of the books in this series you will feel the excitement that will make learning come alive both for you and the children you teach.

Best wishes.

Chris Yapp
Head of Public Sector Innovation
Microsoft Ltd

Authors' acknowledgements

Thanks to all the staff at Cramlington Community High School, in particular the ICT support team, and to the science department, who are without doubt a splendid bunch of hardworking, enthusiastic, creative and inspiring professionals. It is a privilege to be part of the Cramlington community.

This is to my family and to Jan, my inspiration.
Ken

To my beautiful family, Catrin, Eira and Osian who keep things in perspective.
Fergus

The authors and publisher would like to thank Tricia Neal for contributing to the primary resources referred to in the book and included on the CD-ROM.

Introduction

Monday: first day back after half-term. Strange things are afoot. Some of your teachers are getting to school much earlier, and are disappearing into each other's classrooms. Oohing and aahing can be heard coming from open windows. The headteacher has been seen leaving his office and wandering the corridors of the science block. Hands folded calmly behind his back, he pauses occasionally outside the laboratories, before returning to his office with a perceptible spring in his step.

Yes, the interactive whiteboards have arrived; complete with speakers and snazzy pen that let you write on them too. Word is out that there is one in every science lab. You can't wait until Wednesday – science with Mr Quimby. Apparently he can now write on the board without even having to stand up!

▌ICT will transform your teaching

It can! But it won't automatically do so overnight. Having a lot of ICT in a classroom will not miraculously turn a good teacher into a great teacher, or an OK lesson into a great one. In fact, unless the use of ICT is well thought out, it can turn a good lesson into a much poorer one, most often because the teacher has tried to incorporate ICT features and activities at the expense of pace and efficiency. While there is no doubt that having access to an interactive whiteboard coupled with the internet has the potential to bring the outside world into the classroom and therefore make teaching more engaging, we have to carefully consider the best way to use whatever resources we have.

ICT must not be used simply because it is there. Irrespective of the level of resourcing, the driving force behind the progress of ICT inclusion must always be a focus on learning. A coherent and structured approach where learning is the focus during all stages of lesson preparation must be adopted.

In this book, we will share great examples of teachers using ICT effectively, but will view these tools as part of a tried and tested successful model of teaching and learning. The Accelerated Learning Cycle, outlined in the first chapter, is based on years of best practice research into what is effective teaching and learning. It provides a framework that allows us to focus on the uniqueness of the individual including their own learning preferences. It also caters for the way individual learners access and process information and can help teachers operate from the basis of an understanding of the brain and the way it works together with motivational theory.

Our objective is to share ideas that have been successful in many schools, across years and, indeed, in various subject areas, to show how ICT can be used to make the learning of our students more fun and engaging, to promote higher-order thinking, facilitate the promotion of useful life skills and assist with assessment – all of which are the underpinning principles of effective teaching and learning.

The impact of ICT on learning

There is no evidence to suggest that ICT has had any real impact on learning and achievement.

Anthony Gregorc, phenomenonologist

With respect to my esteemed colleague, there is no evidence to suggest that the pen or pencil has had an impact on learning – does that mean it hasn't?

Robert Sylwester
Altercation at a conference on brain-based learning – California 2000

There has, however, been a great deal of research recently carried out on the impact ICT has on education. Sensibly, a number of LEAs in the UK have called for meaningful evidence in order to decide on how to best advise schools on spending their budget, and this call has been met in rigorous fashion. In 2003, Becta (British Educational Communications and Technology Agency), which is the leading govermental agency for ICT in education, published a series of reports aimed at accumulating, analysing and summarizing from current research the impact ICT can have on, among others, motivation, and the effects of using ICT in science. On the basis of Becta's analysis, the reports make the claim that ICT can have positive effects on student motivation and in the teaching and learning of science. These include:

General benefits

➡ Online learning engages demotivated and disaffected students (Duckworth, 2001; Passey, 2000; Harris and Kington, 2002).

➡ Improved confidence, motivation and self-esteem particularly for children with special educational needs and disaffected students (Passey, 2000).

Benefits for teachers

➡ ICT allows teachers to engage and motivate pupils to a greater degree (Betts, 2003).

➡ The internet increases access to authentic data (Osborne and Hennessy, 2003)

➡ Simulations enable teachers to show experiments that would not otherwise be possible (Mcfarlane and Sakellariou, 2002).

➡ ICT provides quicker and more accurate data collection, saving lesson time and giving better quality results (Osborne and Hennessy, 2003)

➡ Students are generally more on task and express more positive feelings when they use computers than when they are given other tasks to do (Becker, 2000).

➡ Amount of off task behaviour significantly decreased during computer and classroom sessions, following the use of multimedia programs for reading and spelling (Van Daal and Reitsma, 2000).

➡ Using digital video as part of learning tasks improved behaviour and on task concentration (Reid/BFI, 2002).

Benefits for pupils;

➡ Visual modes of presentation aid understanding of concepts and processes (Trindade et al., 2002).

➡ Instant feedback enables pupils to refine experiments and hypotheses (La Velle et al., 2003).

➡ Students found learning in a technology-enhanced setting more stimulating and student-centred than in a traditional classroom (Pedretti and Mayer-Smith, 1998).

➡ Students who used educational technology in school felt more successful in school, were more motivated to learn and had increased self-confidence and self-esteem (Software and Information Industry Association, 2000).

➡ Electronic communication enables pupils to become part of a community of learners (Mcfarlane and Sakellariou, 2002).

➡ The mechanical aspects of practical work are reduced, allowing pupils to concentrate on interpreting and analysing data (Mcfarlane and Sakellariou, 2002).

WEBSITE

A full breakdown of this research can be obtained from www.becta.org.uk but a brief summary of the findings is that students who use ICT with a clear focus learn and perform much better than those where the focus is lacking. Not exactly rocket science, but this further enhances the need for effective planning of the use of ICT and an effective teaching and learning framework.

What ICT have you got/do you want?

At Cramlington Community High School we have seen the use of ICT evolve over a number of years, from the days of each department having one computer on a trolley, to our present situation where we have an interactive whiteboard with speakers in every teaching space, web designers, a desktop publisher and an audio-visual technician.

One question consistently asked by teachers at the school, whenever faced with the dilemma of how to spend money on ICT, is 'What can we do with this new ICT that we can't with other resources?'. The starting point for any new initiative must always be to ask the question, 'What positive impact will this change have on the learning opportunities for our students?'.

It's very easy sometimes to be blinded by science. New, attractive looking, innovation-promising software can be seen as desirable when first encountered, but in effect may turn out to be of dubious use and value for money. Technology should not be used for technology's sake. This must never be the driving force behind any innovation. If you can do it just as well with paper and a pencil, then do. Technology exists, and should be developed, to serve teachers and students.

There are a huge number of science specific resources available, each with their own merits and detractions, that it would be ridiculous to attempt even a minor sweep here. The plethora of websites and CD-ROMs providing interaction and information on literally everything needs some reckoning. In the activation phase chapter, you will find useful strategies to use with students when evaluating websites and deciding whether electronic resources are worthwhile or not.

All the ideas in this book were created, adapted and hijacked with two things in mind. The first and most important, how can we enhance the learning experiences for our students? Secondly, how can we employ ICT to enable this? So regardless of the access you have to ICT, you will find, in all chapters, great ideas that you can adapt for use in your own situation.

WEBSITE
CD-ROM

To accompany this book there is a CD-ROM, the role of which is to act as a portal to the organizations and resources described at the end of the connection and activation phase chapters, as well as throughout the book. To make it easier, these resources are highlighted in the margins of the book with the words 'CD-ROM' and 'WEBSITE'. The word 'CD-ROM' indicates that the resource being referred to in the text is actually located on the CD-ROM. The resources on the CD-ROM are organized in the same way as in the margins of the book, that is, each has a chapter number and corresponding letter. The word 'WEBSITE' indicates there is a shortcut on the CD-ROM to the website referred to. Again, these are organized on the CD-ROM by chapter.

Chapter 1
Accelerated learning

In this book, we advocate a four stage Accelerated Learning Cycle for planning effective use of ICT. Many readers will be familiar with the four stage Accelerated Learning Cycle as described by Alistair Smith et al. (2003), which is based on the following key principles:

➡ Recall is dramatically improved when information is regularly reviewed.

➡ Learning is greatly enhanced when the whole brain is engaged.

➡ People access information through all their senses.

➡ People do not learn effectively when placed under negative stress.

➡ People remember context rather than content.

➡ People learn in different ways.

➡ Learning evolves through exploration, mimicry and rehearsal.

➡ Learning happens when students can see the benefits of learning for themselves.

➡ Learning thrives on immediate performance feedback and space for reflection.

At Cramlington Community High School, we try and infuse the principles of accelerated learning into our lessons on a daily basis using the Accelerated Learning Cycle. All of our lessons are planned using this template which contains four stages:

➡ connection phase

➡ activation phase

➡ demonstration phase

➡ consolidation phase.

The cycle is underpinned with the principles of accelerated learning, but above all we use the cycle to plan fun, active and engaging lessons!

▌ Connection phase

In this phase, the aim is to orientate the learner to learning. The connection phase can be thought of as being made up of a number of key elements:

➡ creating a supportive learning environment

➡ connecting the learning/big picture first

➡ agree the learning outcomes.

Creating a supportive learning environment

 You cannot dream with a clenched fist.

Confucius

In order for learning to take place, it is important that your classroom is a pleasant, stimulating and safe place to be – safe not only in terms of absence of physical threat, but emotionally safe too. Your classroom needs to be the kind of place where it is OK to get things wrong and be stuck, where the students' self-esteem is protected and it is easy to get students into a state of relaxed alertness – the ideal conditions for learning. In this kind of environment, lessons are characterized by praise and positive reinforcement and the teacher can communicate high expectations in a positive way, and the students can feel confident, relaxed and are ready to be taken to the edge of their comfort zone.

Getting the physical environment of the classroom right is also extremely important – the room should be a bright, stimulating, interesting place to be. The most effective learning spaces we have seen are laboratories devoid of clutter with staff using the environment flexibly, for example, teachers arranging tables to create a floor space to lay out a standard operating procedure that students have agreed upon. The space could just as well be used for circle time, to practise role-plays or to construct models of ideas.

On a recent classroom visit, the teacher had set-up the environment so that different areas were in use for different activities – one area was used for a written based activity, another to watch a cartoon video through the interactive whiteboard, while the PCs in the classroom were used for students to carry out research. A portable whiteboard was used to guide students on a task.

Creating a safe, supportive learning environment is essential

An example of a colourful and effective display was observed in Julia Shanks' room which included student generated mnemonics to remember the order of the planets.

While a lot of student work is used for display purposes (a clear indication student work is valued), it is important that the display is not dated and should always be relevant to the content of that particular lesson or module.

Connecting the learning/big picture first

This is where the learning is made personal, by connecting what the student is about to learn to prior learning experiences. The student can see the whole picture and where today's learning fits into a bigger chunk of learning.

At Cramlington Community High School, we have a whole-school policy of 'bellwork' – work that begins at the sound of the bell. This could be an activity that is handed out to the students as they come in or a question or thinking game – see the connection phase chapter for a range of activities.

Agree the learning outcomes

To share learning outcomes effectively, we need to translate them into accessible, student-friendly language. We have seen a range of effective strategies used at Cramlington Community High School to share learning outcomes and success criteria. On a recent tour of the science department, we took a digital camera to capture the language that teachers were using to convey the learning intentions. Learning outcomes were clear, on display throughout the lesson, with a range of strategies being used.

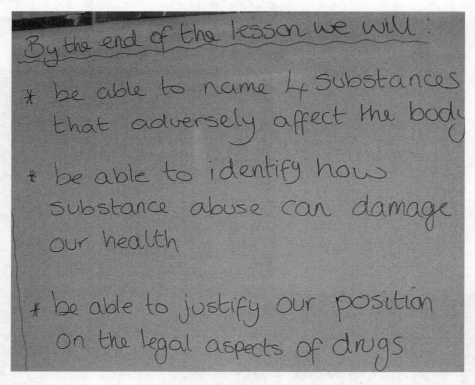

Display learning outcomes at the start of each lesson

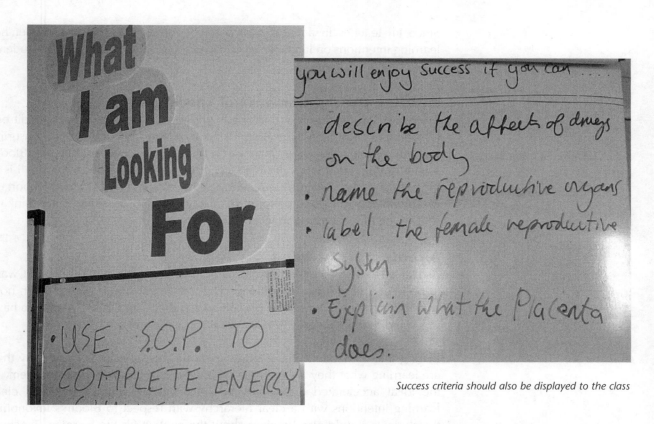

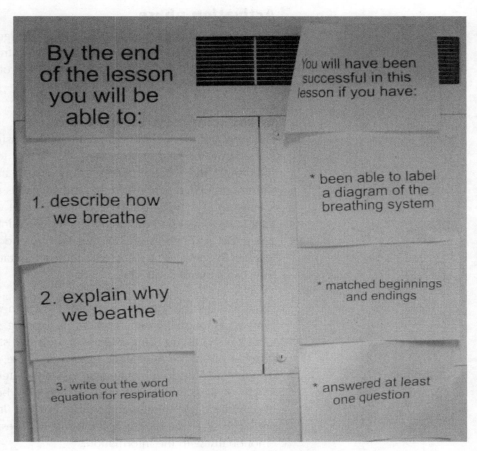

Success criteria should also be displayed to the class

An example of a teacher using clear and unambiguous learning objectives, containing both learning outcomes and specific success criteria, was displayed in a lesson taught by Jill Travers:

Combined learning outcomes and success criteria in one

Since Jill teaches in a number of different rooms, she had printed out her learning intentions on large pieces of paper and displayed them for the students to refer to at all times.

Ensuring the right amount of challenge

To ensure that higher-order thinking is promoted in lessons we also audit our lesson plans using Benjamin Bloom's taxonomy of 'thinking' (1956), ensuring that our learning objectives increase in the required level of thinking. Bloom separates thinking into six distinct categories. Simple knowledge or recall is at the bottom of the taxonomy and although this is obviously extremely important for students to be able to perform in an exam, Bloom considers other thinking skills to be of greater importance.

A context for learning

As teachers, we also often have to participate in meetings that we don't want to be in and find ourselves asking, 'What's in this for me?'. This is often how students can feel about school or particular subjects and this is where we have to try and tune into Radio WIIFM (What's in it for me?).

During the connection phase, students should be allowed to know why they are learning what they are learning – how relevant the learning is for them. In the ideal accelerated classroom, as well as using very explicit and clear learning intentions with a clear hierarchy with respect to Bloom's taxonomy, the students should also be clear about the context for the learning. Teachers who are more successful in this regard often use WILF (What I'm looking for) and TIB (This is because) type of learning objectives.

Activation phase

During the activation phase, we want to engage the learner and involve them in making sense of the new learning. We introduce new information to the students to help them to begin to solve the problems that we have posed and construct meaning.

Introducing new information

Humans access new information all the time using their five senses, yet in most classrooms in the UK, teachers mostly try to stimulate auditory (through speaking) and visual (using good visual aids) senses. At Cramlington Community High School, we try and access as many of the senses as possible – How are the lungs like a fairy cake? Well, it will help if the students have a fairy cake to feel and pull apart as they are thinking about it, so we give them one each! As often as possible we will try and access all of the senses in our lessons. Recently, on a study of rainforest habitats, the students were given kiwi fruit slices to taste and smell.

What will get the students engaged? How can we hook them into the lesson? Can we emotionally engage them by tapping into the 'Wow' factor? This is what we should do using a range of tools and strategies. In essence, this is the 'teacher bit' of the Accelerated Learning Cycle, which is extremely important, it should be purposeful, but engaging – about ten minutes is our recommended length of time. ICT has a huge part to play because of the immense visual impact the right stimulus materials can have. In the activation phase chapter you will find lots of examples using ICT designed to engage the students emotionally with the information.

This activation section of the cycle is where the students try and make meaning of the new information, where they process the new learning internally, each in their own natural way. At Cramlington Community High School, having completed a learning styles analysis, our students are aware of their own learning preferences – they know how they learn best. As a result, we are very explicit about how the activity we want the students to do will access a range of learning styles. Over the course of a number of lessons we will ensure that students get the chance to learn in their preferred learning style. In the same way, we are explicit that students also need to learn in ways they prefer less – that we want them to develop a range of strong learning preferences and become well rounded learners.

Demonstration phase

This is where students get a chance to show what they know, and that they have been successful versus the learning outcomes and success criteria. Real understanding involves 'transfer' of knowledge to a different context – a recently recorded interaction between a student and teacher at Cramlington Community High School demonstrates the need to apply new learning to different contexts. In their intermediate GNVQ science exam, a student had become stuck on a question on photosynthesis of seaweed. After the exam, the student complained to the teacher about her difficulty with this question:

Teacher: *'Why did you get stuck? You are great at photosynthesis, you aced it in the mock.'*

Student: *'Yes, but we only did trees and plants, we never covered seaweed.'*

In the demonstration phase of the cycle, students are given opportunities to generate products that demonstrate their understanding. Using ICT tools the students can communicate this through a range of feedback opportunities. By getting feedback from the teacher or other students in the class, the learners' thinking can be fine tuned. The demonstration phase should not just be about answering practice questions – which certainly has its place – the demonstration phase should be highly interactive, rich in opportunities for educative feedback and, above all, student centred.

Consolidation phase

This is one of the most important stages of the cycle, and often one of the most overlooked. Too often teachers leave an inadequate amount of time for carrying out a full review, either because they are reluctant to interrupt students while they are fully engaged in the activity section or they want to ensure students finish the task. In doing this, the students are missing out on an essential part of the learning experience. It is during the review that we get students to:

➡ step back and reflect on the learning experience

➡ review the key learning points

➡ teach them memory techniques that will endure and will be useful beyond school

➡ reflect on the process of learning (debrief)

➡ preview the next learning steps.

It is extremely important to focus not only on *what* is learned but *how* it is learned, and we are very explicit about this in lessons with our students at Cramlington Community High School.

Chapter 2

The connection phase

Introduction

You are a Year 7 student, taking your place in a line outside your new science classroom. Your first science lesson of the year. Your teacher appears at the door and an expectant hush descends. Invited into the class, you scramble for a seat on the second row – don't want to be on the front, too swotty; not too far back as you don't want to be wearing your glasses the whole time. Keen to make a good impression you settle in to your seat, put your wet coat on the back of the chair, get out your pencil case, and arrange your sparkling new scribing instruments, as the rest of the class pile in and do the same. Mr Quimby finishes a conversation in the corridor with the French assistant, before he moves to his desk and says, *'Don't take anything out just yet, I'm going to give you your seating plan. Get your stuff and line up at the back.'* *'Oh for goodness sake,'* you can't help but mutter under your breath.

Of course, Mr Quimby has the hearing ability of a fennec fox. Looking to assert his authority he leaps at the chance to make an impact and you are the unfortunate one he picks on to make an example of to the rest of the group. Your name has been noted. You have been identified as a troublemaker. You have now taken an instant and permanent dislike to your new science teacher. And you used to love science at your old school.

Having eventually settled in to your new seat, which you hate compared to the one you had chosen, the Quimster, as he will come to be known, now invites you up to receive your new numbered textbook. All 32 are issued in the same way.

One year later...

Now beginning Year 8, you do not have high expectations for your new science teacher. All science teachers are idiots as far as you are concerned. The class is not forming an orderly queue outside the door and quite frankly you don't care. Your new teacher has come to the door to invite you in. Mr Hanzo refers you to the whiteboard, onto which is projected a plan of all the seats in the lab, with each student in the group allocated to a specific seat.

Front Desk

Danielle	Jamie		Paula	Callum	Nicola	Bert		Lauren	Stephen
Lionel	Stacey		David	Hannah	Marwood	Megan		James	Andrew
Karl	Rebecca		Daniel S	Rachel	Daniel M	Elizabeth		Adam	Jenny
					Amber	Scott		Hank	

Seating plan displayed on the whiteboard

Locating your seat, you are grateful for the organized start to the lesson and really appreciate the fact that your name is up on the board and spelled correctly. Bert breathes a sigh of relief, as he likes to sit near the front so that he doesn't always have to wear his glasses. You're thinking, with this considered and pre-prepared seating plan, Mr Hanzo has arranged the class without the students being given any reason to have to think themselves or that anyone has been placed with any intent. No one has been singled out for special treatment.

Welcome – your first topic this year is about microbes. See if you can answer these questions:

What is a microbe?

What is a vaccination?

How do vaccinations protect you against diseases?

Write down the name of five different diseases.

Introduce new topics with a few short questions as a starter activity

Greeting you all individually as you pass through the door, with a welcome and a smile, Mr Hanzo hands you a slip of paper. You all seem very clear what it is you are expected to do. All the students check for their name on the board, move to their seats, settle in and begin to work on the task the teacher has just given them. The highly visual seating plan disinclines anyone to argue about where they are sitting, and besides, most students seem to be focused on the problem they were given on the way in. You are thinking, this science teacher is really serious about learning. The whole process of students finding their new seats, in a new classroom, has taken less than two minutes.

When you are all settled, Mr Hanzo tells the class that you have as long as it takes for the music to finish, to consult with your neighbours to refine your answers. Without another word he clicks on his computer and Peggy Lee's 'Fever' starts to play. Very clever, you think to yourself, a highly relevant song to accompany the starter activity. And, recalling it's roughly three minutes, it lasts an appropriate length of time to focus the thinking and allow group discussions. As it is a song that most of the class recognize, you realize straight away how long you have to complete the task, and set about it with an uncommon verve. The countdown clock that is displayed on the whiteboard assists your time keeping.

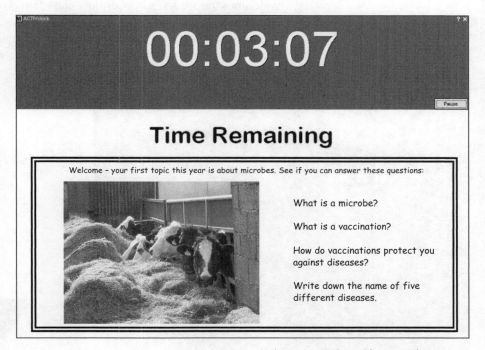

Keep an eye on time with a countdown screen

In less than six minutes, you and your fellow students have found your new seats; had a pleasant interaction with the new teacher; attempted to answer some science questions which really got you thinking about the new topic; worked on your own intrapersonally and then in small groups interpersonally; and had relevant auditory stimulation. You are ready (though you are probably unaware of this) to provide your new teacher with valuable feedback from the starter activity, carefully planned as a bit of pre-assessment which will give an indication of what individuals and the class know about the new topic. Misconceptions will be highlighted at an early stage. This activity enables Mr Hanzo to plan and adapt the subsequent lessons in the topic to take account of prior knowledge. It was particularly useful in this case as last year your class was visited by Bert's dad, a medical expert in tropical diseases.

Fortunately, your new teacher is now aware of this and will not be repeating content you already know. You are thankful for this as you often find yourself saying, *'but we did this in primary school – twice'*. You are still not sure, though, why six Friesian cows appear to have a cameo on the starter activity. After a little while you can bear it no longer and ask: *'Sir, why are there six Friesian cows on the starter activity?'*

'Finally, I thought you'd never ask', replies Mr Hanzo. A lively discussion ensues, spearheaded by Bert, on the role of cows in the development of Edward Jenner's first vaccination attempt against smallpox. You have a fuzzy feeling and a suspicion that this is going to be a great year for learning science.

ICT tools for supporting the connection phase

Effective use of ICT to create a supportive learning environment

The first thing you may wish to do with a new group is to begin to set-up the community of learners, and it may not be appropriate to have a seating plan in this first lesson. In this instance, why not create a simple slideshow that welcomes the students in your new class. This would be really encouraging for students – especially our younger charges who may well be feeling apprehensive. Simply put each student's name on a separate slide with a common background, and set the slideshow to scroll every few seconds.

Create a supportive learning environment by engaging your students

Images could be added, perhaps as a background, which allude to the new topic to be explored. These images could even be used to assign students to their working groups for the day. *'All daffodils over here please; could the swans move to Hannah's table; Bert, could you corral the horses?'*

When setting up the learning experiences for your students, it is important to consider both the emotional and the physical environments. It is important that you get the students to buy into the lesson right at the start, so an engaging and stimulating activity should be offered at the outset. This activity should provide an opportunity to see success at this early stage of the lesson, which will provide motivation for the rest of the learning experience.

The activity may, when appropriate, relate to the previous lesson you shared with the class. Your students may have had 15 or more lessons with other teachers by the time they get back to you. It is reasonable to expect that they will need some kind of activity or stimulus to get them back into the swing of things. If a new topic is being covered, then an activity like Mr Hanzo's cow slip can be employed.

Easy seating plan

Using Publisher and PowerPoint to create and display the seating plan for a class really takes no longer than handwriting a seating plan. The beauty of doing it in this way is that, in subsequent lessons, should you wish to amend the seating plan, you do not need to rewrite the whole thing again. Simply swap a couple of names around or add a table or two. Handy when you have to move classrooms as well.

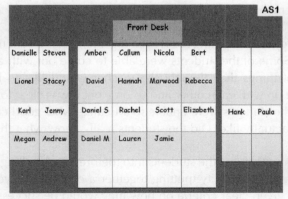

AS1

		Front Desk					
Danielle	Steven	Amber	Callum	Nicola	Bert		
Lionel	Stacey	David	Hannah	Marwood	Rebecca		
Karl	Jenny	Daniel S	Rachel	Scott	Elizabeth	Hank	Paula
Megan	Andrew	Daniel M	Lauren	Jamie			

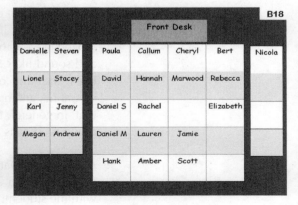

B18

		Front Desk				
Danielle	Steven	Paula	Callum	Cheryl	Bert	Nicola
Lionel	Stacey	David	Hannah	Marwood	Rebecca	
Karl	Jenny	Daniel S	Rachel		Elizabeth	
Megan	Andrew	Daniel M	Lauren	Jamie		
		Hank	Amber	Scott		

Electronic seating plans make amendments fast and easy

Having a seating plan on your desk is a great way to learn students' names, which is essential for building a community of science learners.

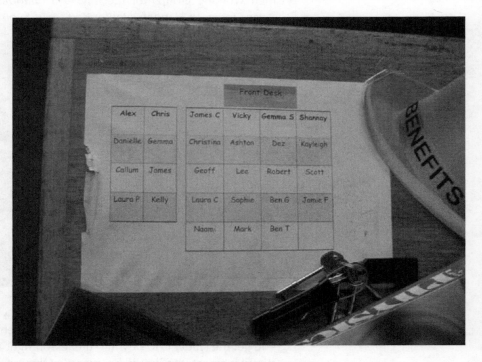

CD–ROM Ch2/Resource 1

Another useful application of PowerPoint is the random name generator. An example is included on the CD-ROM. This resource helps teachers to implement a no-hands-up policy – an essential assessment for learning strategy to ensure all students are engaged. Change the names to those of your class and away you go!

Digital cameras

It is possible to use ICT as a way of managing student behaviour. The rationale is that kids like ICT and 'if I sit student "x" down in front of the computer, he will sit there and not disrupt others'; that is, as long as he isn't looking at porn on the internet and isn't causing any bother.

Can ICT actually be used to promote better behaviour in students? Can a digital camera do this. At Cramlington Community High School, this strategy is used frequently. Faced with hard, photographic evidence of their miscreant behaviour – and the camera never lies – even those students who use the good old, 'it wasn't me' routine, will be forced to concede that they were being less than perfect during an activity. The use of the digital camera to promote good behaviour originally came from one of our own teachers, Darren Mead, who was trying to emphasize to his class the importance of working more collaboratively in groups. He asked his class what good scientific group-work looked like – if they were working really well together, what would this look like and sound like? Some of the students were able to come out with a few sound bites, the kind of things they thought the teacher would like to hear – co-operating, getting on with each other and so on – but it was clear to the teacher that, in general, the students were unable to articulate what good collaborative group-work was actually like. Did the students really know what this meant?

At this point, Darren then got the students into their regular working groups and set them off on a timed activity (putting together a quick rock cycle display), with the students given clear criteria on how they would be successful. Instead of circulating round, getting in among the students with his usual vigorous enthusiasm to ensure that they were focused and on task, Darren chose to step back a little and simply use a digital camera to photograph what was happening on a group by group basis. At the end of the tightly timed task, Darren quickly asked the students to evaluate how they had done versus the success criteria, and then asked them to gather round the interactive whiteboard. In the meantime, Darren had uploaded the images from the digital camera via a USB cable and used them to emphasize the difference in performance of two of the groups in the class.

Group 1: This group were extremely successful in their task, meeting all of the success criteria by not only including downloaded images of all of the rock types within the display but also keywords showing how the rock was formed and three examples of each type of rock. Darren showed the class some photographs of the students at work, the images really capturing a collaborative and supportive ethos. He asked the rest of the class what the pictures showed:

 They look as if they are listening to each other.

They're looking at the member of the group who's talking.

They look like they're all working, even if they're doing different jobs.

They're working together in pairs on different parts of the display.

Darren then showed the class the images gathered from another group, who had enjoyed a significantly less successful time than Group 1.

Group 2: This group were successful in meeting only half of the success criteria. The images gathered also captured the working mood of the group and, again, Darren asked the rest of the class what the pictures showed:

 Two of the students are cutting out paper and the other two are sword-fighting with rulers.

Two of the students are reading from a textbook, while the other two are on the computer – is that a games website?

Did the four of them sit down together at all?

Only two of them are working at any one time.

While, initially, the two students who were less on task than they should have been found the hard evidence a little amusing, their looks became more sheepish as more and more of the images were shown. To end the lesson on a positive note for these boys, Darren promised that next lesson he would take more pictures of the boys at work in science and that he was confident that he would also be able to use these images as a good example of quality collaboration and group-work.

At the beginning of the next lesson, Darren showed via the interactive whiteboard the images of the successful group working together from the previous lesson. He then asked students to pair up and write down a set of group guidelines on what good group-work would look like and sound like.

Darren then gave the students another timed group-work activity he had designed for the lesson. In this lesson, all of the groups worked extremely well together, all completing the task successfully and Darren was also easily able to celebrate the work of the two boys who had let themselves down previously, their level of effort, motivation and behaviour having increased dramatically.

Having shared his experiences with the science department, we have since all used the digital camera in a similar way in the classroom. One teacher even found that the threat of presenting a few pictures of one student's off task behaviour to his parents at the forthcoming parents' night to be an excellent motivator to promoting good behaviour!

Using a digital camera to aid practical work and emphasize laboratory safety

At Cramlington Community High School, we try and put scientific enquiry at the heart of all of our science lessons and therefore encourage our students to participate in practical work as often as possible. As a science college we are well equipped with science equipment and large laboratories, which means that even with our regular class size of 28, whole-class practicals are a regular feature of the department. What is difficult with large class sizes is demonstrating to the whole class how to set-up the experiment. It simply does not work having 28 students gathered around a side bench to look at a practical set-up, which means that the teacher usually has to use up valuable class time in repeating the demonstration for smaller groups. What our teachers have successfully done to ease this problem is to use digital cameras to take snapshots of the practical set-up and project these onto the interactive whiteboards, often using images from different angles on a rolling PowerPoint slide. With the image of the practical set-up magnified on the large interactive whiteboard, students can refer to this simply and often.

Using pictures as a reminder of the last lesson

Reminding your class what happened in the previous lesson through pictures of the students at work, can be a very powerful starter. Use of questioning is important at this stage to make the most of the pictures.

Review of practical investigation from previous lesson

What was Lionel doing here?

Why?

What stage of the separation was he at?

Can you offer any advice as to how he might improve his technique?

Yes that's right Bert, Lionel could have used a test tube rack to rest his funnel in.

What is this process called?

How does this technique work?

Can you think of a way to collect the water that is lost?

Which group set this up?

Why is it not being supervised?

Effective use of ICT to engage students from the bell

Drag and drop

Another effective review starter to a lesson is to employ the 'drag and drop' facility on your interactive whiteboard. This type of activity does not require an interactive whiteboard. Drag and drops can be created using software such as Word, Excel and Inspirations. Hardware options to enhance the practicality of this activity without purchasing a interactive board could be a tablet PC or a device such as Mimee, which makes your normal whiteboard interactive.

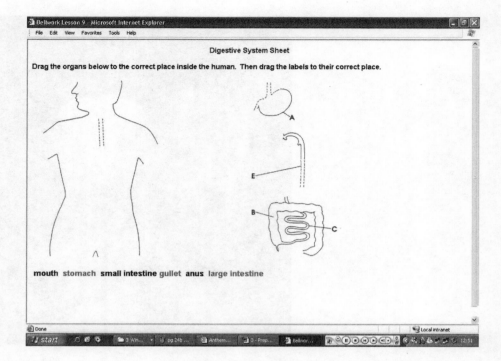

In this Key Stage 3 activity, parts of the digestive system and labels appear on the board. Again, students share the pen between them and attempt to complete the diagrams by adding labels. The images were simply scanned from Heinemann's Spotlight Science resource file and separated using imaging software such as Photoshop or Paint Shop Pro.

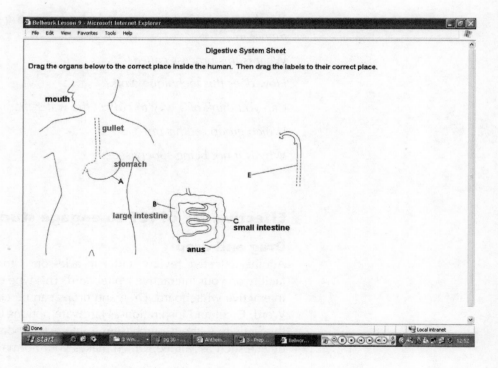

This activity can also be simply achieved by using PowerPoint, but the interactivity is lost when the slide is viewed full screen.

WEBSITE

Interactive activities

Many topics in science lend themselves readily to a quick interactive review at the beginning of a lesson. To prepare the following, a screenshot was taken from the GCSE specification website (www.aqa.org.uk), copied onto a PowerPoint slide, and a whiteboard pen used to annotate over the top of it.

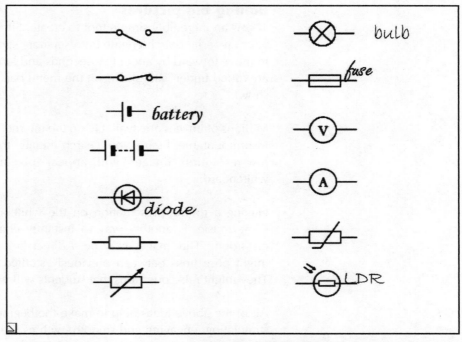

A simple and easy interactive activity to start off a lesson

The interactive whiteboard pen was then given to the first student who walked into the classroom. They were asked simply to label any one of the components on the board. On completion, they had to pass the pen on to another student, and so on. More than half the class ultimately had the pen, with some of them choosing to pass because the components they knew had already been taken. This was a great starter for several reasons.

Observing the class as they did this activity (which took only three minutes) was useful, giving an indication of which students knew their component symbols and which students did not. The ones left unanswered clearly needed to be revisited and the ones that were incorrect, for example, the 'cell' labelled as 'battery', allowed misconceptions to be addressed.

When the majority of the class had come in, some students had taken their books out and started to look up the symbols. Others were arguing and trying to recall some of their electronics learning from technology. In the end, one student had taken charge of the pen and was being prompted by others to amend some of the answers in a different colour.

This short and simple activity had a significant number of students engaged from the outset. The way in which they unconsciously assumed different roles, whether they were generating answers, researching, motivating others, taking the lead or staring out of the window, provided useful information for the future, when students might be organized into groups for practical work and challenges, in which they need to make use of, or develop, different skills and dispositions.

This type of activity is generally self-managing, requiring little input from the teacher at the beginning of the lesson. It leaves you with a moment or two to check in with individuals, have a quiet word with one or two students if need be, and observe the dynamics of the group. Time to manage the beginning of a lesson in effect.

Rolling big pictures

This is an incredibly simple tool to create. Simply copy and paste images from your favourite search engine onto separate slides in PowerPoint. Set the slides to move forward by about five seconds and loop continuously. These functions are found under 'slideshow' on the menu bar, in 'slide transitions' and 'set-up show'.

Millions of images are available on the internet and the sheer number can seem insurmountable. Refine your search initially to look only for large pictures, as low-resolution images will appear pixelated when projected onto a whiteboard.

Having a rolling presentation on the whiteboard, perhaps accompanied by some music, is another way to instantly engage students as they enter the classroom. The images may be a direct link with the lesson to come. They might pose links between previously studied material and the new content. They might raise questions that students will want to find out more about.

All of the above ideas help to make the beginning of your lessons purposeful, stimulating, engaging and smooth, with as little dead time as possible. With a positive start to the lesson, your students are more likely to engage well with the rest of the learning cycle.

Using music and sounds

The use of music to contextualize a lesson right at the start begins the learning process as students walk through the door. The choice of music could be an obvious link, or it could be more obtuse, requiring students to have a guess at the focus of the lesson. This idea of using music to kick-start a lesson is not a gimmick. For example:

Peggy Lee, 'Fever' (microbes)

The Cadillacs, 'Speedo' (rates of reaction)

Queen, 'I Want to Break Free' (changes of state)

Fun Lovin' Criminals, 'Smoke Em' (effects of drugs)

Jah Wobble's Invaders of the Heart, 'The Sun Does Rise' (Earth in space)

Monty Python, 'The Galaxy Song' (universe)

John Shuttleworth, 'Save the Whale' (human impact on extinction)

Tight Fit, 'The Lion Sleeps Tonight' (food webs)

Music can be used to great effect in this way. It can often remove the need for the teacher to make any kind of verbal signal that the attention of the class is required. Simply standing in a prominent part of the room as the music fades can signal to the class, in an entirely non-confrontational manner, that the next part of the lesson is about to happen. We use this device a great deal in our lessons, as do many of our colleagues. It really makes for a positive start to a lesson.

Apart from making links and stimulating thinking, music can also be used as a timing device. We are all familiar with television and radio programmes that use music or jingles in this way. We have become conditioned, as part of daily life, to expect something to happen when we hear a certain sound. How would we know the news was about to be read on Radio 4 without the pips? Would the late Richard Whiteley have had the gravitas he did without the closing ticks of the *Countdown* clock? Would he have even known when the time was up?

These are examples of events happening when music or a sound stops, but sounds also signal the beginning of events – the starter pistol of a race; or the warning boom of a foghorn; or a combination – the warning of a start: to prevent parents of young children from setting about their own televisions with an uncommon verve, the BBC, in a generously spirited public health warning fashion, gave the most irritating show on the air the most grating theme tune. Offensive and unacceptable to adult ears, the first second of *The Tweenies* signals to parents of small children across the UK that it is time to head for the safety of the kitchen and an extended cup of tea.

Music to set a calm tone
Assuming Jamie Oliver's philosophy has not quite infused into your kitchen staff, you have probably come to expect rather a range of behaviours and attitudes after lunch. Some of our more sugar and caffeine enhanced darlings may need that extra little stimulus of relaxing background music to ease them into their afternoon's learning fare. Try the following:

> Satie, 'Gymnopédie'
>
> Delibes, 'Flower Duet'
>
> Norah Jones, 'Come Away With Me'
>
> Chis Isaak, 'Wicked Game'
>
> The Connells, '74-75'
>
> Beethoven, 'Fur Elise'.

Music to pick up the pace
On those days when your class has already peaked after a bowlful of Sugar Puffs for breakfast, and without resorting to stand-up and the dancing girls, you might need some livening up tunes to go with some Brain Gym®. How about:

> Mozart, 'Eine Kleine Nachtmusik'
>
> The Mock Turtles, 'Can You Dig It'
>
> Elvis Presley vs JXL, 'A Little Less Conversation'
>
> Mikis Theodorakis, 'Zorba's Dance'
>
> Mas Que Nada, 'Sergio Mendes & Brasil '66'
>
> Jools Holland, 'Enjoy Yourself'.

Music is a great memory hook – two tales

Case study 1

Mr Moon, Mr Moon
You're out too soon
The Sun is still in the sky
Go back to bed
And cover up your head
And wait 'til the day goes by

My four year old is a great fan of the outdoors. I took her and her brother to some woods near us. Once there we decided to sing a few songs, one of them being her aunt Bethan's favourite, 'Mr Moon'. We have since been to numerous other arboretums where we perhaps were less vocal. Nothing of particular note happened on the walk, but to this day she refers to those woods as the Mr Moon forest, while not having a name for any of the other woods we have visited. And two years on, when she hears that song, she let's people know that there's a Mr Moon forest near her house.

Case study 2

During a revision session with my Year 11 tutor group, a few weeks before exams, we were sharing ideas about different ways to revise. The notion of using songs came up and Christina, in an unusually lucid moment, related how she still remembered a song she and her classmates learned to review the rock cycle with Mr McKnight, back in Year 9. She was able to sing it and could even expand on the content of the song. She reckoned that teachers should allow time in every lesson to review in this way, but Kelly disagreed. She did not rate a musical review highly, remembering only the panic that she felt that she may be asked to perform her composition in front of her peers.

There are two valid points here. All students are individuals and what works for some will not work for others. Students often remember context over content. But music is clearly a very powerful memory tool. Think of how many songs we know off by heart, more than we probably realize. And doubtless some that we would rather not know, particularly irritating but catchy snippets from advertisements. How many of us can remember the 'Shake and Vac' advertisements or can still recite the lyrics from the 'Um Bongo' ad?

Advanced warning

Try this. At the beginning of a lesson, inform the students that their task at the end will be to create a review song encapsulating the salient points of the lesson. This should keep them thinking throughout the lesson about what to include and how to condense their understanding. It will develop creativity and flexibility as new learning points are developed. They will be compelled to constantly assimilate and review the content. In a longer lesson you might give a couple of minutes to allow groups to add to and adapt their compositions. And hey, it's fun.

Keeping it real with help from cross-curricular links

To guarantee engagement we must make our science real for our students – show how it always relates to real life and why it is a great idea that we study it. Remember, a large proportion of our students often fail to see the relevance of studying science. Putting it in to context, and engaging them emotionally with the history and the people, is an excellent way of getting and keeping them onside. The above lesson introductions will relate directly to English and history, and should help to put the science into context. Students may question the relevance to science here, but that would be a great thing!

A variety of these techniques could be used over a series of lessons on this topic. Returning to the same content, through whichever means of engagement, focuses and refocuses students on what they are studying, particularly if you have not seen them for a few days. Input such as this at the beginning of a lesson allows students to return to the learning, recap and focus in their own time and in their own way. It can serve as a reminder if it is a topic that is being developed and is a very effective context creator.

While we want to engage our learners in their learning we do not want to over stimulate them. Sometimes less is more and by removing a stimulus, sight or sound, we in fact concentrate our attention on fully utilizing those senses that are being addressed. When thinking of how to liven up a series of lessons on the Haber process[1], how about playing just the sound of a bombing raid from street level, or an assault on a trench? Even just the audio track, without the visual of the beginning scenes from *Saving Private Ryan,* would certainly engage even the most reluctant students. The noises of panic, fighting and explosions without the imagery that usually accompanies them in film and television, leaves a lot more to the imagination. If appropriate, perhaps add one of the many poignant poems from the First World War. For example, this poem by Wilfred Owen (1921) could be displayed and slowly developed against a plain background on a whiteboard.

Anthem for Doomed Youth

What passing-bells for these who die as cattle?
Only the monstrous anger of the guns. Only the stuttering rifles' rapid rattle
Can patter out their hasty orisons.
No mockeries now for them; no prayers nor bell,
Nor any voice of mourning save the choirs,-
The shrill, demented choirs of wailing shells;
And bugles calling for them from sad shires.

Poem by Wilfred Owen

Similarly, visual footage could be shown without the accompanying sound. This would allow more visual learners to interact with the context of the subject.

---

[1] The Haber process was developed by Fritz Haber shortly before the First World War, and its industrial scale preparation allowed Germany to produce ammonia in bulk. Ammonia is an essential ingredient for making fertilizers and explosives. The development of this process effectively kept Germany in ammunition and food, prolonging the war indefinitely.

Connecting

To avoid lost time at the beginning of a lesson, you can display 'bellwork. This is a term we use at Cramlington to mean a starter activity that is commenced on the sound of the bell. This is a starter activity that students can begin literally 'on the bell'. It will usually be a short activity that connects them back with their learning from last lesson. Or maybe some exemplary work submitted by students from that group, which they produced last time or have emailed to you in between science lessons. Simply having the bellwork on the board in a highly visual display, means that those students who arrive first have something to do straight away and it frees you up to greet your students at the door and set a really positive tone for the lesson. Slideshow submissions can be condensed into one presentation, moviemakers can be cued up, digital pictures of poster presentations can be displayed, or even a collection of the best questions, comments and bloomers from the previous lessons can be shared – some of these ideas, public displays of learning and working together successfully cannot help but get your students onside and motivated.

▌ Agree the learning outcomes

Introduction

Your headteacher has had a tip off that Ofsted will be popping in this half-term for a little inspection. In assembly, he explained to the students, primarily, you suspect, to ensure teachers actually do it, that each and every lesson would now begin with the learning outcomes being shared with the class. You think this is a good idea but are not really sure what all the fuss is about. Mr Quimby has taken the message on-board and conscientiously writes the outcomes up. A typical start to his lessons following that assembly would be:

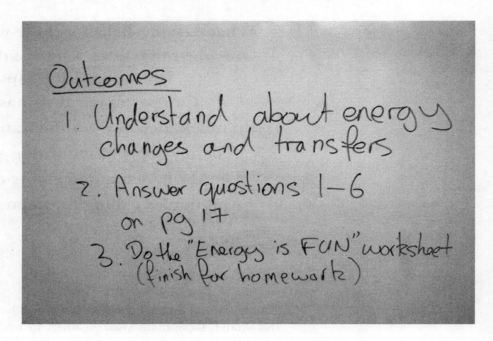

A week later, another lesson:

Mr Hanzo is once again covering for Mr Quimby. He has the outcomes written up on the board but has covered them with a piece of flip chart paper.

Engage students from the moment they step into the classroom

As you enter the room, some wordless, pensive tune is playing in the background and a slideshow of various news flashes is projected on the board. These are screenshots of various articles and headlines from newspapers and journals published on the internet. Mr Hanzo must have spent a couple of minutes getting these together beforehand – fair play to him.

 We're going to be finding out about the factors that affect the populations of species. I'd like you to write one question or something that you found interesting from the slideshow on a Post-it note that you'll find on your tables and then pop it on the question wall.

Ninety seconds later…

 Let's have a look at these, there are some really important questions. Here are just a few:

How come there's all this talk of cod shortage, but there's always cod in our chippy?

If the world is getting warmer, how come it might end like in the film The Day After Tomorrow, *all covered in snow?*

Does it really matter if that little dragon thing in the picture gets extinct?

Eels are disgusting man, what's all the fuss?

If whales are eating all the fish, why don't we just kill all the whales, then there'll be more fish for us?

Why have I suddenly got loads of snails in my garden, and most of the year there are none at all? I keep stepping on them!

Now this is a great question! I think we should add this one to the outcomes for today and we'll attempt to answer as many of these over the next week or two. I'll pass these questions to Mr Quimby so he can follow them up with you next time.

Let's have a look at the outcomes for today.

We will be successful today when we...

- Arrange some species into a food chain and state some of their adaptations (everybody)

- Create a food web which combines our different food chains (all together)

- Use the food web to decide how the populations of certain species will be affected when we remove other species from it (most of us)

- Begin to explain some factors that affect the populations of species (some of us)

- Explain why Bert's snails are out in force now and not for the rest of the year (everybody – sharing ideas for a review)

Success criteria

You can see that Mr Hanzo has a rather different idea of what outcomes are compared to Mr Quimby. You have a really good idea about what you will be doing in this lesson and can see that you should be able to do some things that you could not do before – especially the snail question. It's nice, you think, that one of the student's questions has been included prominently – you have a sense of ownership of the lesson. And Bert is well pleased that he's up on the board.

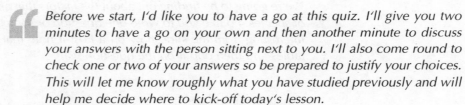

Before we start, I'd like you to have a go at this quiz. I'll give you two minutes to have a go on your own and then another minute to discuss your answers with the person sitting next to you. I'll also come round to check one or two of your answers so be prepared to justify your choices. This will let me know roughly what you have studied previously and will help me decide where to kick-off today's lesson.
Any questions?

Sir, what if we don't know any of them?

Don't worry Bert, this is so that I know to revisit any essential knowledge that perhaps you haven't covered or have forgotten, before moving on to look at the factors that affect population changes.

What do we have to do then?, calls out Roger.

Mr Hanzo has projected the quiz up on the board and explains clearly to the class exactly how to fill in the sheet, pointing to the columns he is referring to. This, you note, is much easier to follow than if you just had the sheet in front of you.

Will this short activity also help you to put us into appropriate groups, sir? asks Bert.

Yes, replies Mr Hanzo.

	First attempt (show what you know)			Second attempt (after three lessons)		
	True	False	Not sure	True	False	Not sure
1. Herbivores eat only plants						
2. Humans are omnivores						
3. All food chains start with the top predator						
4. The arrow in a food chain represents the transfer of energy						
5. A producer uses photosynthesis to make its own food						
6. A pyramid of numbers is always shaped like a triangle						
7. The second level in a food web is always a secondary consumer						
8. When more predators enter a habitat the number of prey will decrease						
9. Some plants compete for sunlight						
10. I can name five factors that affect the population of some species						
11. I can name ten factors that affect the population of some species						

A simple way of finding out what students do and don't know

Sharing exemplar work and discussing success criteria

We often set our students off on a task where they have a required outcome. They know what they have to produce and what specific content and understanding they have to show to succeed. But how often do we share with students what a really outstanding example of learning looks like? Many students find it difficult to relate the marking criteria of, say, coursework to their work in progress. Showing them some exemplar work can really help to demystify the assessment process that their work will be subjected to, and let them see what success really looks like.

There are many places where teachers can obtain exemplar resources to share with their students. The most obvious, and often the most useful, is the school in which they work. A large department may have a huge range of excellent past coursework that can be uploaded onto the school network. Teachers could print these out so students can see the marking scheme that their work is marked against.

Internet cheat sites – great resources

There is no point in hoping our students will not be naughty and attempt to obtain illicit coursework from internet sources. Only recently I had a student who handed in a piece of coursework based around an experiment we had not even done! One of the chemicals had been the same but there the resemblance ended. Many of us will be familiar with students who have turned in work that clearly has not been written by them. Cheating has become easier with the availability of internet access with most schools and many families having broadband access. We, as teachers, should not ignore or shy away from this latest technological advancement, but embrace it, utilize it and champion it. An interesting activity to do with students is to download examples of previous work and ask them to mark it against the marking scheme. They might well find these pieces of work are less then exemplary!

▌Resources

CD-ROM Ch2/Images D, E
WEBSITE

DNAinteractive – explore the DNA revolution
www.dnai.org/index.htm

Howard Hughes Medical Institute, produced and distributed by The Red Green and Blue Company

This is a DVD resource containing four hours of movie files of interviews with leading scientists, including 11 Nobel Laureates, exploring the journey of discovery of the structure of DNA. The struggle to discover the nature of life's building block, including false starts, successes, applications, implications and the ethical questions that arise from an understanding of DNA, are all addressed here in small, digestible chunks.

This resource really comes in to its own because of the quality of its animations. They are stunning and have been produced to the highest quality. They are extremely helpful when introducing this often very abstract concept to students. The animations can be viewed and played without sound, but the resource also offers auditory commentary at two different levels, basic – ideal for a GCSE audience, or advanced – aimed more at A level biology and chemistry students.

CD-ROM Ch2/Images N, O, P
WEBSITE

Powers of ten
http://micro.magnet.fsu.edu/primer/java/scienceopticsu/powersof10/

This is one of a few high quality websites that look at the powers of ten. Combining models, artists' impressions, satellite photos, digital camera photos as well as a selection of micro- and sub-microscope images, students can travel from the very edge of the universe, a distance of 10^{23} metres from Earth, through the solar system and down through genes, atoms to the level of quarks.

This is a great resource for discussing standard form, logarithms, the need for prefixes and the sheer scale of the breadth of study science has to offer. This site has also been used very successfully in our maths department, who pounced on it when introduced to it. A great site for the 'Wow' factor.

CD-ROM Ch2/Image Q
WEBSITE

Brainpop
www.brainpop.com

Quite possibly the most used resource in our science department. This American, subscription based website, offers very short, simple animated movies on literally every topic that could possibly be covered in a science curriculum, as well as plenty on health and social issues. Accompanying the movies are short interactive quizzes which students of all abilities and ages are always happy to participate in. The movies, just three or four minutes long, are perfect for introducing, reviewing or prompting a discussion to find out what students already know or what they would like to know more about.

WEBSITE

A compendium of resources
http://science.nhmccd.edu/biol/animatio.htm

This site contains links to over 100 other websites that contain animations, simulations, movies and tutorials on all sorts of topics. It really saves time on searching for a new stimulus. The job of searching has been done for you. It is a great place to start. It contains sections on anatomy, ecology, geology, animals, plants, biology and physics.

WEBSITE

Alta Vista audio and video search
http://www.altavista.com

This is a search engine every bit as good as Google, but it offers excellent audio and video searches. If you are looking for a sound effect, movie clip, part of a specific song or a video of a science demonstration, this is your best starting point. Some LEAs have barred blanket access to this valuable website because of copyright issues, but it can also be accessed by teachers at home when planning and resourcing lessons.

WEBSITE

How stuff works
http://science.howstuffworks.com/

This is an excellent website that explains how hundreds of different gadgets and devices, processes and phenomena work. All explanations are accompanied by useful graphics, usually images or animations and many contain useful links to further websites. The site also has a very effective search facility. Examples we have found useful have ranged from how photocopiers work to how viruses work.

CD-ROM Ch2/Image AA
WEBSITE

Delights of chemistry
http://www.chem.leeds.ac.uk/delights/

Professor Mike Hoyland and colleagues from Leeds University are responsible for possibly the best chemistry demonstration lectures in the UK. With a mighty arsenal of practical demonstrations they have won over many audiences both at universities and as guests in schools. In this website they have gathered a video library of many of their best demonstrations. The reason this site is so effective is that a thorough explanation of the chemistry involved is offered to accompany the video. Teachers looking for ideas and demonstrations for all ages, topics and abilities will find more than enough to inspire them for a year's worth of delightful chemistry. And if you can't do the practicals in your teaching space, you can show students the video.

WEBSITE

Define
www.google.co.uk

A nifty function of Google is when you type 'define' into the search box. This is not a science resource in particular, in fact people from any walk of life could usefully benefit from this device. If you want a couple of different ways of explaining a certain term – for example, homeostasis, simply type 'Define: homeostasis' and Google will instantly search the web for definitions of the term. These will usually range from very simple explanations to quite high level expositions.

This is useful for giving a bit more insight in to certain areas. The website from which the definition is taken is also accessed by a hyperlink, so that you can easily access the context in which a definition was created. More often than not, clicking onto these links produces even more information that might be of further relevance to your cause.

Using digital photographs

WEBSITE

www.haworth-village.org.uk/nature/time-lapse/thumbs.asp

The Haworth village website has wonderful nature photographs and excellent time-lapse images that can be displayed on a whiteboard for discussion and annotation. The majority fit into the science curriculum and offer the opportunity to discuss processes that are difficult to observe. For example, eleven months in the life of a laburnum, the full moon, frogspawn developing or just the beauty of a plant flowering.

Planet Archive – the Noah's Ark for the online era

WEBSITE

www.planetarkive.org/home.html

This website has a large database of the world's creatures in it's Fact File. Each data file includes a still photograph and often a short video of the animal in it's natural surroundings.

Strings

WEBSITE

www.google.co.uk

Students are frequently asked to do research. Often their first port of call is the internet. We know there is far too much information out there and the process of sorting through it to locate appropriate content can be mind numbing. A recent activity prompted a student to want to find out exactly how many wind turbines would yield the same amount of energy as the current amount of fossil fuel used in the UK. Using inverted commas at either end of the search criteria means that Google will check only for sites that contain the exact phrase. This example gave the student a good starting point: 'How many wind turbines would be needed'. The following are just a few of the search results to be located that could prove to be useful:

Scoop: Wind energy report released

How many wind turbines would be needed to get a 20 per cent market share for wind? Based on existing turbine technology, about 800 to 2000 turbines would be ...

WEBSITE

www.scoop.co.nz/stories/PA0505/S00351.htm

Research-TV

10:01:41:20 SOT: Professor Oswald: – 'If we work out **how many wind turbines would be needed** in Britain just to power our cars through hydrogen the answer...

WEBSITE

www.research-tv.com/stories/society/bonds/transcript/

[PDF] GCSE Science Double Award Modular Physics Modular Module 9 ...

File Format: PDF/Adobe Acrobat
10.1 At a certain wind speed, a wind turbine transfers 2500kW from the wind. **How many wind turbines would be needed** to replace a 1000MW power station? ...

WEBSITE

www.aqa.org.uk/qual/gcse/qp-ms/AQA-346009-W-QP-Nov04.pdf

Chapter 3
The activation phase

▌ Input

I'm going to introduce you to one of the greatest cultural and scientific achievements in the history of mankind, was Mr Quimby's opening gambit.

Is it the wheel? offered Bert.

Well, not really...

The internal combustion engine! continued Bert.

That wasn't what I was thinking of either.

Pasteurization?

Bert!

Keeping a watchful eye on Bert, Mr Quimby went on to share his understanding of how John Harrison's chronometer changed the face of sea transport. Talking rather quickly so as not to be interrupted by any irritating questions, particularly from Bert, he went on for a full 50 minutes. He was particularly pleased that he could still hold the attention of a class for an entire lesson without resorting to any visuals, something the younger teachers seemed unable to do these days.

15 minutes in, your mind starts wandering back to the science lesson last week that Mr Hanzo covered for Mr Quimby. You were in the middle of a module that looked at different systems in the body. In the previous lesson, in an out of character moment of lucidity, Mr Quimby gave you a preview of what to expect next lesson. You would be learning about breathing, which he said was all about respiration. Not used to being given such forewarning you made sure you did a little research of your own beforehand.

Over dinner at Bert's house the night before, your suspicions that respiration was not really about breathing were confirmed by Bert's dad, who also shared, in no uncertain terms, what he thought of Mr Quimby.

You were pleased when Mr Hanzo showed up. As you entered the lab he gave you a big blue disc of card. Everybody got a card. Some were blue and some, including Bert's, were red. Others got smaller cards with O_2 or CO_2 written on them. The tables were laid out in a long line right down the middle of the room. This looks interesting.

On the whiteboard was an animation of a person breathing, showing the position of the lungs. After explaining what he hoped you would be able to do at the end of the lesson, Mr Hanzo took you on a visual journey ever deeper into the lungs.

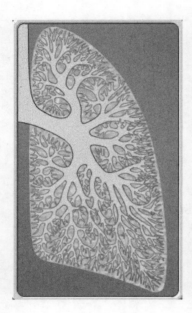

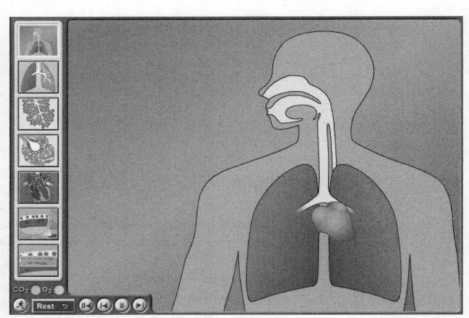

Breathing and respiration teaching tool

He explained that when you breathe in, the air is sucked into your lungs, down the trachea, through the bronchus and in to the bronchioles. Although he was using a plastic model as well as the images on the board, some of the class couldn't match all the parts of the lungs. In response to this Mr Hanzo clicked forward a page and a prepared slide came up with the labels on.

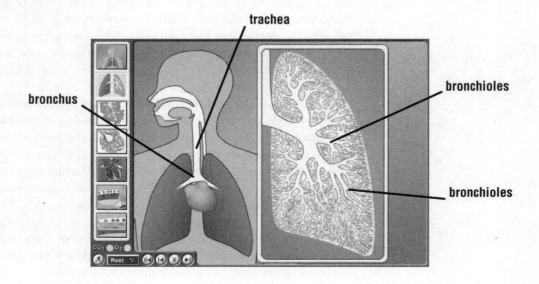

We then went on to look at how the oxygen we need for respiration actually gets in to our blood.

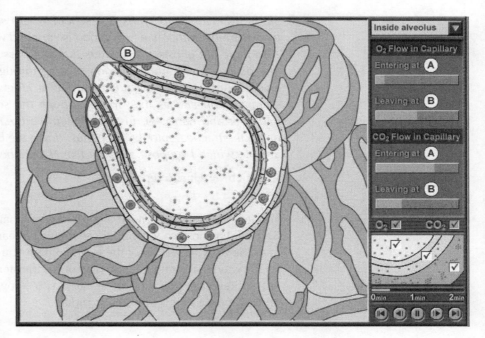

Alveoli teaching tool

You could see the individual gas molecules of oxygen and carbon dioxide moving across the capillary boundaries in both directions. You were even able to control the breathing rate of the model using the animation and could switch off sections of the lung or types of molecule so that you could focus on specific parts. Mr Hanzo then produced a broccoli and, reminding you of the animations, asked you the following questions:

How are the lungs like broccoli?

How is respiration like Hogwarts from *Harry Potter*?

After some consideration Bert came up with a good response to the second metaphorical question.

Sir, is it because Hogwarts is a school where students are enriched in their learning, rather like how blood is enriched with oxygen in the lungs. Also there are ghosts at Hogwarts that can pass through the walls, a bit like oxygen and carbon dioxide passing through the thin walls of the alveoli. And when the students arrive at Hogwarts they enter a large entrance hall and as they move through the school, the corridors get narrower and narrower, just like when we breathe in air and it passes down the trachea, into the bronchus, down the bronchioles and into the alveoli, which I suppose are a bit like Harry's bedroom.

To which Mr Hanzo replied, *Yes.*

You feel as though you have a good idea of what goes on inside the lungs. But Bert still has no idea what all those pictures mean. Fortunately, you now move in to the activity section of the lesson where you use the cards you were given on the way in, to act out a role play of the transfer of gases in the lungs. Though not so keen on this type of activity, you know Bert will get a really good understanding in this kinesthetic model.

Using ICT to help introduce new information

Enter the Rain Forest, the London Underground, or Heathrow Airport...

Sometimes we might like to create an environment into which our students will be immersed for some time. Many of our students, particularly our youngsters, will have limited experience of the world. ICT can help make initial connections and put learning in to context. It can help make the abstract more concrete. The internet has numerous places where image and sound files can be downloaded. Animations and videos are easy to get hold of as well. Simply enter your requirement into your favourite search engine, stating what format you are looking for (MP3 or WAV for example), and an endless list of resources will be displayed. Most of these will be entirely useless, but you usually find an acceptable match on the first page or two of search results.

CD-ROM Ch3/Resource 2

Making images relevant to classwork using microscopes, digital cameras or digital video cameras, provide resources for recall, discussion and presentation. You can find sample images taken by children on the CD-ROM that can be used on their own to introduce or reinforce a topic.

This is a cheap and inexpensive way to locate and integrate digital resources. Obviously there is a copyright issue here. In the same way that we should not photocopy from textbooks or novels, we should not download, store and share digital material, whether it be images, movies, animations, sounds or music, without the owner's consent. There is a large amount of material that can be legally used for educational purposes, but it is the reader's job to ascertain whether this is so.

Plan together

The plethora of resources available on the internet are useful only if you can think of an effective way to incorporate them into the learning experience. This is where collaborative planning is really important. You may have a great idea for a lesson or how to use a particular resource. But sharing that idea with a colleague or two will realize other ways of moving forward. In teaching, two heads are always better than one. A resource that you have just discovered and think is great, may well be in use already. Indeed, some of your colleagues may have a better idea tucked away. This was constantly happening in our school. It seemed like everyone was spending more time than was necessary looking for resources and planning lessons.

So we tend to take responsibility, often in pairs, for planning and resourcing a specific topic or series of lessons. Our timetable has been structured to build in two hours of planning and professional development each week, to allow for among other things quality lessons to be planned and placed on the science intranet site. Because we do not need to plan and resource every lesson that we teach, we are able to create really good learning experiences, knowing that other colleagues are preparing the same for us.

Have a shared area

A school intranet or, more easily set-up, a shared network area that all teachers can access from anywhere in the school, makes life a lot simpler, and can mean that the onus of producing high quality lessons is shared among the department.

This is the digital solution to having 'schemes of work' folders in the preparation room. Lesson plans can be gradually digitized and the electronic resources are hyperlinked into these documents. This is an incredible time saver for many reasons. The online lessons can be constantly added to and enhanced without the need to be rewritten. If you happen to have an inspirational INSET from a thinking guru or the assessment policy in your school changes, then a limited amount of work need be done by amending or adding to your lesson plans.

Of course, the students will benefit from an accessible intranet too. Perhaps they have been off sick. Whatever the reason for their absence, with the lessons accessible online, they can catch up with what they have missed, explore any multimedia resources and preview the next lesson. With a fully established intranet, it should reduce the frequency of the mantra, 'I haven't done it cos I wasn't here!'

Radio programs

Auditory learners, which we all are to some extent, can benefit from an excellent set of resources available online for free. Most of the big media networks have a digital archive of programmes, some stretching back for years. Science specific content is often well regarded and therefore readily available. BBC's Radio 4 has a huge selection of programmes to search through.

Practically every topic taught at secondary level can benefit from radio input. These programmes are created for an adult audience, though usually a scientifically literate one. Most productions are therefore readily usable with Key Stages 3 and upwards.

I recently used an audio clip from an American chat show where two 'experts' were discussing the combined effect of an expanding population on the world's diminishing oil reserves. At the beginning of the clip a fabricated newsflash from 30 years into the future was read out. This painted a pretty bleak picture for the Year 10 students, many of whom started to be extremely concerned as they realized that the situation could become very worrisome in their own lifetime. This was a great emotional hook through a medium they were not used to interacting with in this way.

No matter how stimulating the subject content, without some kind of outcome from a listening exercise the students will not be compelled to actively engage with it. The simplest of graphic organizers, a page that the students can doodle on as they listen, jot down questions and then create some order from what they have heard, really serves to focus their thinking. Giving students a blank piece of paper is a recipe for stress, confusion and poor responses, leading to a discombobulated class of teenagers. By providing them with a graphic organizer, such as this one, no matter how simple it is, you provide a structure and expected outcome – things that are important to students.

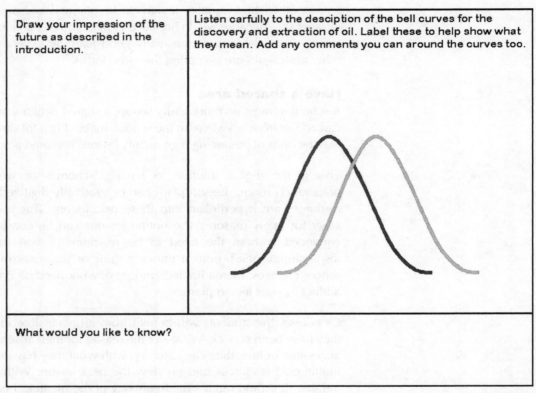

Draw your impression of the future as described in the introduction.

Listen carfully to the desciption of the bell curves for the discovery and extraction of oil. Label these to help show what they mean. Add any comments you can around the curves too.

What would you like to know?

Graphic organizer

Students were given this simple graphic organizer so they could record ideas and jot down any questions in an orderly fashion. They also had to translate a description of a graph. This task was differentiated. Some students were given the bell graphs and simply asked to label them, while others had to interpret the description given on the radio show entirely by themselves and generate their own graphs. This worked well as the students had an opportunity to discuss and compare their results.

Bring an expert teacher into the classroom – screen capture

These mini movies are very simple to create, needing only a small, cheap microphone connected to your computer. Screen capture technology is an excellent and cheap way to spice up introducing new information in your classrooms. Software such as ScreenFlash and Camtasia allow you to record exactly what is happening on your computer. They record sound and importantly the mouse movement. So it is very useful for creating tutorials for using software applications, for example.

This technology will be discussed in more depth in the demonstration phase chapter. Indeed, it was the developers' intention that these software would be used for students to demonstrate their understanding. More information can be found on their websites.

Setting cover work

There will always be the need to set high quality cover work when teachers are absent. Often we do not know who will be taking the lessons. Frequently, though, they will not be other science teachers. A short tutorial followed by a brief guide through the activities and resources to be used in the lesson would be an excellent way of bridging the gap. These can often be prepared well in advance and take the form of independent study. Pupils are given a task and the resources necessary to complete the task successfully without being reliant on a science teacher. These stand-alone lessons can be prepared and resourced in advance and kept in an accessible place on the school network and then employed when emergency cover is required.

Often your students will seem overjoyed when they discover their teacher is off, as it can be an excuse for an easy lesson, when not a great deal needs to be done. A high quality, fun, step-by-step guide through the learning outcomes, introduced by a virtual member of the department, can help to win back the hearts and minds of our potential strays.

Bringing the internet in to a non-networked environment

Even if your school is not networked and internet access in your classroom has not yet arrived, there are various ways to 'import' the delights of the world wide web. If you have access elsewhere, these ideas can be employed depending on your requirements.

We have mentioned screen capture technology. This is particularly useful if the content you wish your students to interact with is on an extended web page where you have to scroll through it, or a very simple animation is worth sharing.

Screenshots are the easiest way to take information from the internet. The 'Print screen' button (usually found at the top right-hand side of your keyboard) literally copies what is on the screen, minus the cursor. These images can then be popped into a slideshow for presentation purposes.

Audio and video files can be downloaded usually by right clicking on the hyperlink that starts the file and selecting 'Save target as'.

There are many superb animations on the internet, which cannot, unfortunately, be recorded with screen capture technology or a still image screenshot. In these cases, it's a matter of making a note of the weblink to the animation in question. Remember, though, that websites are highly transient creatures, and where one day your lesson plan had a link to a great animation or web page, the next day that website might not exist. We have noticed this quite frequently when a lesson is accessed the year after it is written; sometimes the links are no longer available. If you want to make sure a particularly useful animation or website is always available then a web designer, network manager or a member of the IT department may be able to assist.

WEBSITE

Brainpop

Although we are not advocating specific products in this book, we feel that www.brainpop.com deserves a special mention. This is without a doubt the one resource that the science department uses on a regular basis. Perfect for Key Stages 3 and 4, short (two to three minute) animated cartoons give a brief synopsis of the fundamental points of practically any scientific topic in the curriculum – tectonic plates, food chains, AC and DC current, microbes, reaction rates. This has recently become a subscription site due to its popularity, but at the time of publication you can trial it before you commit – and it is easy to do so too. Give it a whirl. The only problem you may encounter is getting your bursar/LEA to deal with an American company.

Obviously there is an endless number of websites and CD-ROMs providing information on literally everything under the Sun. On page 72 of this chapter, you will find some suggested strategies for how students can select appropriate information. But, as teachers, we would benefit from considering some of the questions in the table on page 73 when looking to use websites to introduce new information in our classrooms.

Digicam

With much of the new information being shared with a class through a whiteboard, it makes sense that certain practical demonstrations could make use of this too. David MacGowan introduced the idea at Cramlington Community High School of using webcams to present small-scale practicals on the whiteboard. You can pick up a decent webcam for just a few of your department's pounds and the benefit will be real and immediate.

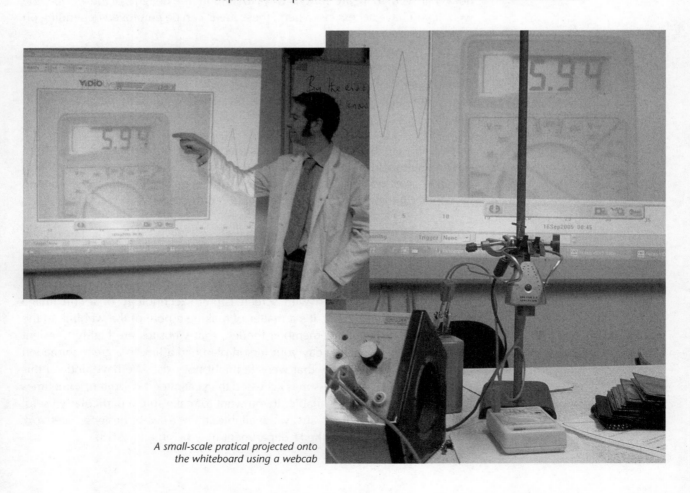

A small-scale pratical projected onto the whiteboard using a webcab

Often a whole-class demonstration is desirable, due to time constraints, but rarely does everyone get a good view of what is happening. These simple devices plug in to your projecting monitor through a USB port and allow you to display everything that is happening live through the whiteboard.

An even cheaper option is to get a security camera from B&Q, for example. These offer even better quality imaging, though they are bulkier and likely require a firewire port or some other adaptor.

Picoscope

Although we are not advocating specific hardware or software, we feel this device warrants a special mention. It is a very cheap alternative to a cathode ray oscilloscope. Again, it is almost impossible to run a whole-class demonstration with everyone getting a good view of the CRO screen. A digicam could be employed to get around this problem. But how about turning your computer into the CRO itself?

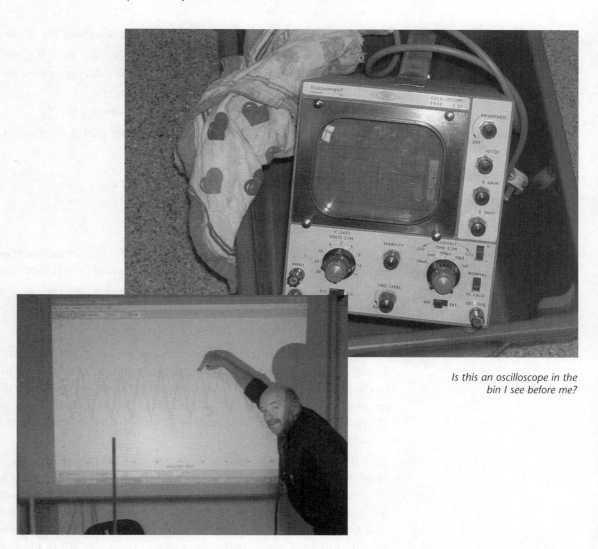

Is this an oscilloscope in the bin I see before me?

The picoscope is a small scart size (scart = a 2 pin socket) device which is plugged into the back of a laptop. It is then simply connected to a signal generator.

Activate with Mr Quimby

Right Year 9, now that we have seen how particles behave from the double page spread in the textbook, it's time for you to do a practical.

The technician brings in a tray with some ice cubes on it.

Gather round while I demonstrate the experiment for you.

As you plod to the front of the lab you suspect that this will not be one of the most enlivening of science lessons.

First, bring your beakers to me and I will give you four pieces of ice and a thermometer. Take them back to your seat and, in groups of three, put 20 cm³ of water into the beaker. How could you make sure you got just the right volume?

Could we use a 20 cm³ pipette, sir?

A measuring cylinder will be fine Bert.

But to be really accurate...

Then you need to measure the temperature every minute for 40 minutes.

While you are recording your data you can start to write up your practical. Remember to include your aim, prediction, apparatus, method, results and have a go at the conclusion too.

Sir, I think we did this experiment when we were in Year 5.

And don't forget to do a graph of your results and a diagram of your equipment. Off you go.

Activate with Mr Hanzo

Right Year 9, we've just been discussing why it is important that scientists have a good understanding of changes of state and how particles move.

Yeah, that little Camtasia video Year 11 made for us was really provocative and interesting – I can't wait to find out more!

Thank you Bert, I shall pass on your appreciation.

Could I have one person from each home group to the demonstration bench to set-up the experiment. You guys will have to explain to the rest of the group what it is you have set-up, what the equipment will do and present and describe what the graphs produced at the end show, so that the rest of the group will be able to work out what is going on in terms of particle motion.

So I have a bit of a mystery for you to consider. We will look at the heating and cooling curves of some different substances. First, I would like you to make a prediction of what you expect the graphs will look like for water being heated from ice at -5°C, and being heated right up to 105°C. Discuss in your groups for two minutes and agree on a graph. Be prepared to justify your particular graph. While you are doing that, the 'experts' will be setting up the temperature probes with the data-loggers, which should plot some heating and cooling curves for us. We will be encouraging ice to melt, heating chocolate gently from room temperature until it has melted and heating and then cooling this waxy substance called stearic acid.

The data-loggers will plot the graphs for us, but while the experiments are going on, each and every one of you will be asked to come and read to me the temperatures from the glass thermometers that will also be in the substances. Although data-loggers do the dull stuff, it is still useful for you to be able to take accurate readings from the thermometers. I have chosen three thermometers which have different scales on them to keep you on your toes!

Before the changes of state are complete you will need to do some research on particle motion. There is a range of books from the library and science department, as well as these websites that you are welcome to use too. When you have the printouts from the data-loggers you have the opportunity to present the ideas and information you have discovered using your research resources to explain the shapes of the graphs, and comment on how they are different from your predictions – use the ideas from the research you have just been doing. In your group, try to explain why these flat areas on the curves are present. You can annotate your graphs with writing and diagrams to help you explain.

Are there any key words we should be looking out for Mr Hanzo?

Thank you Bert, yes. You must include the term latent heat with a useful explanation. You have 30 minutes, but spend a few minutes at the beginning deciding who will be doing what within the group and discussing each of those roles together.

I will be coming around asking questions and taking photos with the digital camera. When you have completed this activity I will share some of your ideas and explanations by displaying the photos on the whiteboard. We'll find out exactly what's going on and iron out any misconceptions

After all that I will give you a couple of SAT questions from the Testbase database to see how well you can apply what you will have learned. Any questions?

Can we copy the graphs onto the laptop and annotate them on the computer?

Tell you what Bert, I'll drop them in to our group's folder in the shared documents part of the intranet. You still have to be ready in half an hour though, okay.

It'll be a challenge, but I like it.

Right then, could I have the nominated experts from each home group up to the demonstration table please.

The activate stage of the cycle is where the students try and make meaning of new information, where they process new learning internally. Many readers will be familiar with the work of Howard Gardner (1983) on multiple intelligences and may work in a school where the students are aware of their multiple intelligence profile through completion of a learning styles analysis. In more and more schools, students are articulate about their own learning preferences – how they learn best and they know how they learn less well. There is a wealth of information that is potentially now available from these learning style analyses – multiple intelligence profiles, information on the time of day that the student prefers to work in, whether they want the room to be light/dark/hot/cold/quiet/noisy and with or without food and water to hand. For example, see page 52 for a set of data from a class of Year 9 students at Cramlington Community High School.

The data shows the percentage of students with preferences in the following areas:

In terms of the students learning environment

Factor		% preferred		% preferred
Mobility	stationary	25	movement needed	75
Sound	quiet	30	sound/noise/music	70
Light	bright light	55	low light	45
Temperature	cool	60	warm	40
Study area	formal	55	informal/comfortable	45
Motivation	self-starting	55	externally motivated	45

In terms of the learning profiles

Sensory modalities	% of students with a strong preference
Talking/discussing	75
Inner dialogue	100
Reading	55
Seeing/watching	90
Visualizing/imagination	85
Manipulating	100
Experiencing/doing	90

What are the implications of being aware of this information? When would you use it? Is it of any relevance?

Accelerated learning, since its popularization in the late 1990s, has from certain quarters been on the sharp end of some criticism. To many, the theories underpinning accelerated learning are a rehash of something similar that appeared in the 1960s, which eventually died away and as a result has a bit of a 'fad' tag to it. One of the most vocal opponents to accelerated learning has been a former Chief Inspector of Schools, who has consistently disliked the concept of lessons – which are based around the learning preferences or learning styles of the students – describing this as irrelevant and guilty of getting in the way of effective and efficient teaching and learning. Pat Preedy said in *The Daily Telegraph* (2002):

What exactly is a 'Learning preference'?... Can, for that matter, anyone sensibly deconstruct the notion of learning how to learn?... I have never been convinced that we do, as individuals, have different 'styles'. It is more, I think, a matter of different kinds of learning needing to be approached in a different way. And, in any case, if there are 30 children in a class, no teacher, however energetic, is going to be able to structure the lesson in terms of their personal preferences.

There is a point he makes, in that it is impossible to cater for all of the multiple intelligence needs of every child, every lesson, and one should not try to. I do believe, however, that we should acknowledge that students do have different learning styles and that over the course of a number of lessons we should ensure that students get the chance to learn explicitly in their preferred learning style. In the same way, we should be explicit that students also need to learn in ways they prefer less – that we want them to develop a range of strong learning preferences and become well rounded learners.

Like many others, the former Chief Inspector of Schools believes that a good grounding of subject knowledge is what we should be transmitting to our students. The authors of this book, however, remain unconvinced that teaching 15-year-old students about Ohms law or the half-life of a radioisotope will be of benefit to many students (barring the few who make a career down these particular paths) and believe that what may have been the right diet of learning for a student a generation ago may not be the right one for this one. It can be argued that this generation of school children bring a significantly different set of qualities and experiences to their learning than those of previous generations and this alone means we should constantly rethink what we teach and how.

There are pitfalls with adopting an accelerated approach, many of which the authors of this book have seen or experienced. The first trap that teachers can often fall into is that in an attempt to make the lessons multisensory, multi-intelligence, the teacher has done so at the expense of pace, efficiency and rigour. We can think of a lesson where the teacher was trying to teach an accelerated learning lesson on ocean habitats. The students walked in to the sounds of the ocean, with images scrolling past on the interactive whiteboard. The students then went through a series of activities, each to hit a different multiple intelligence muscle:

➡ A guided visualization to imagine what it is like to be in the ocean – *'Close your eyes students and imagine you are a small fish in the sea. What does it feel like? What does it sound like? What creatures can you see? Is there a food chain? How much sunlight gets through?'*

➡ Interactive food webs – students were given different roles and had to organize themselves into a living food web.

➡ Reading – the students had to read a passage on ocean habitats and had to summarize the key points on a graphic organizer.

➡ Poetry writing – the students had to make their own poems on the ocean.

At the end of this 120-minute lesson, the students had certainly had fun and they had flexed all of their multiple intelligence muscles but questions had to be asked about the depth of learning reached and about the length of time spent in class reaching this level of understanding. In this case, the exercising of multiple intelligence muscles was done at the expense of efficiency, pace and rigour and there were lessons to be learned from this. What would have been better to do would have been to put the students through one or two of the activities, exploring the concept in more depth with perhaps some examination questions to demonstrate their own learning.

If used intelligently, an Accelerated Learning Cycle is a highly effective tool to engage students and help them learn better. If it is not used in an effective way, with efficiency and rigour kept firmly in mind, then it could lead to lessons that may be fun, but at the expense of valuable time that most teachers with a packed curriculum to teach simply do not have.

ICT has a big part to play in helping students make meaning of often difficult scientific concepts. ICT can provide students with high impact visual source material for them to interact with, provide virtual laboratories for them to experiment in and with data-logging technology can really help put scientific enquiry at the heart of a lesson.

Effective ICT tools to enhance the activation phase

Using a digital camera to plan out an investigation

We set-up the following set of slides as a teen magazine type story, extremely cheesy, but as you can imagine it hooked the students straight away.

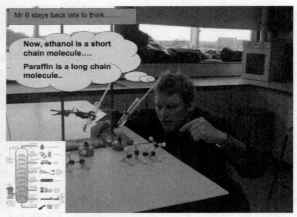

At different points in the presentation the students were asked about the questions on the slides.

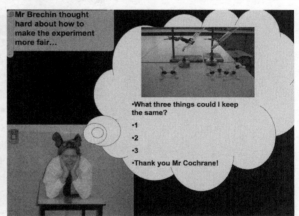

CD-ROM Ch3/Resource 3

Using the slides in the way described helped the students to focus on why they were doing the practical and how to do it safely and fairly. A digital version of this teen photo story that can be edited to suit your needs can be found on the CD-ROM. Why not create your own?

Using a digital camera to tease out scientific misconceptions from students

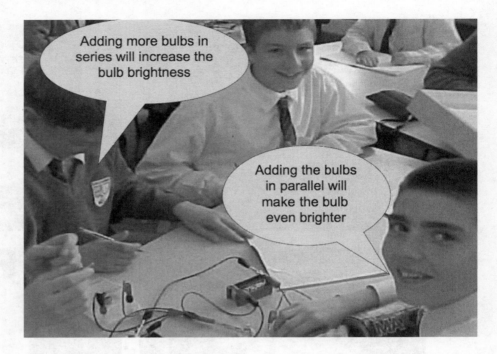

At Cramlington Community High School, we are constantly seeking to promote higher-order thinking within our classrooms. Many teachers are extremely adept at asking probing questions which really promote thinking and a great deal of head scratching from students (the 'Mmmm' factor, as we call it). How do you ensure that the same level of thinking takes place in every classroom? At Cramlington Community High School, we take the issue of planning the questions we should ask very seriously indeed, and share these via our online lesson plans. One method we successfully use to share good questioning practice is by making a series of concept photos available to staff, which also makes simple and effective use of a digital camera. Many of you may be familiar with using concept cartoons from the publication *Concept Cartoons in Science Education* (2000), which contains lots of scientific concepts being discussed by cartoon characters who approach the concept from different angles. A number of teachers have used this strategy extremely successfully, except this time using a digital camera and students to create our own in-house concept photos:

CD-ROM Ch3/Resources 4, 5

There are two examples of concept photos on the CD-ROM that you can edit for your own use, together with a tutorial on how to make your own concept photos.

We have seen home-made concept photographs used extremely effectively by teachers as excellent starter activities in lessons to introduce concepts, establish prior knowledge, but also to tease out the kinds of misconceptions that students have. One highly effective use has been when the teacher has eavesdropped on scientific conversations (or arguments) between students about the science involved in the task at hand and has used a digital camera and PowerPoint to create an instant concept photo, therefore letting the whole class eavesdrop on the argument. In one example, a teacher overheard a discussion between two students, who were investigating how the size of a parachute affected its rate of fall. Two students were putting the case forward to another that when a skydiver opens their parachute, that they go upwards for a little while first. The teacher put a snapshot on the board of the students in discussion (one even happened to be holding an imaginary parachute) and wrote out the key arguments in speech bubbles. When the teacher asked the whole class about who was right, they were shocked to learn that the misconception existed among almost all of the students. The teacher then sensitively asserted that although the arguments of both parties were well delivered, the correct answer was in fact the opposite of what the class believed.

Chocolate teapots

Another extremely effective use of a digital camera is to get students to create their own concept photos in order to display to each other. In a recent vocational science lesson, I observed one of our teachers, Poppy Saltonstall, who wanted to teach students about properties of materials – specifically thermal conductivity, electrical conductivity, hardness, strength and density. The strategy that Poppy adopted was to place students into different groups with each group investigating one property practically. During the practical, the students also had to take a photograph of their work in order to create their own concept photo. Within the concept photo the students had to create conflicting statements about the results of their experiment – one correct statement and two incorrect statements – that would then have to be proven or otherwise by the other groups through investigating that property themselves:

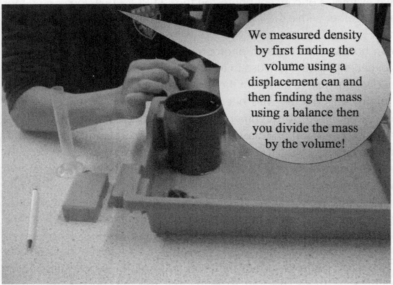

After the students had created their own concept photographs, they then had to investigate another material property. Before they did this they had to look at and discuss the concept photograph created by other students, and make a prediction as to who was correct. I overheard students saying to each other from almost every group, 'I *think he/she is correct because...*' and '*What they are saying is wrong because...*' which is to me the kind of thing I would want to hear from students in science.

Throughout the lesson it was clear that the students were enjoying their learning and were engaged in their work, but the level of interaction and thinking I witnessed in the creation of the concept photographs was extremely impressive, with the students trying to create statements that they hoped would outwit their classmates.

Crocodiles and furry elephants – using ICT to create virtual laboratories

In many science departments around the UK, the majority of good science teachers think of themselves as science teachers first, physics, biology or chemistry teachers second. With teachers assigned their own group at Key Stage 3 and with the majority of students taking double award GCSE science or vocational science courses, teachers are often found teaching outside their specialist science area and aren't confident with this. However, every year when they get their teaching order and they see that the first module they are teaching is electricity, a simultaneous closing of eyes and exhaling takes place. Behind firmly shut eyelids they can picture themselves telling students repeatedly not to hook five batteries in series up to a single light bulb, explaining to the lab techs that a record number of bulbs have been blown this lesson, feeling their eyes strain as they try to pick out a fault in student-made circuits that look like spaghetti, all the while patrolling the class with enough crocodile clips hanging from the tail of their jackets to set off an airport metal detector three times over.

Oh for a laboratory where the batteries never run out, the buzzers always buzz, the bulbs never blow up, there are always enough wires to go around and they never tangle up together, and where students can truly see what happens in series and parallel circuits. Crocodile Clips is a piece of software that provides this virtual laboratory. Easy to use, the on-screen toolbar allows students to select and arrange pieces of virtual electrical kit before adding the connecting wires between terminals by an easy click and drag. Wires can be removed by using the crocodile tool to 'snap' these wires up, which the students really enjoy doing.

What makes this an effective activate tool is that it gives the students a hassle free, 'what if' playground. The teacher can ask questions like, 'What if you add another two bulbs in parallel to this series circuit?' and the students can explore this without the worry of logistical impediments. While the student is experimenting in this electrical playground, they may need some support as to why the bulbs are behaving the way they are when more bulbs or components are added. It is here that another member of the animal kingdom can help the student make connections in this activate phase of the cycle. A great idea for students who are embarking on crocodile clip activities designed by teachers is to simultaneously open up the software package, Furry Elephant, in a separate window.

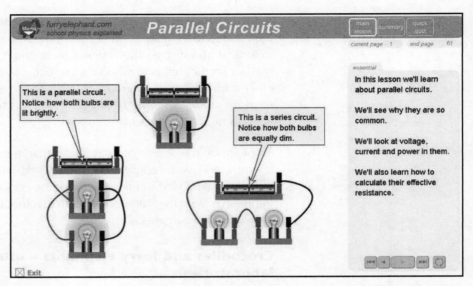

Electricity explained

Furry Elephant is a very student friendly tutorial program which helps to unpack the mysteries of electricity. An excellent teaching resource for non-physicists, the colourful animations and simple explanations could really help a student who is wondering why half of their bulbs have suddenly dimmed.

CD–ROM Ch3/Resource 6

There is a trial version of Furry Elephant's fantastic electricity explained on the CD-ROM. Teachers and students from Key Stage 2–4 will find this resource extremely useful. There is also pre-release access to radioactivity explained for users of this book. These resources provide a structured step-by-step and interactive approach from a very basic level – clearly created by people who know about learning.

Aid packages, rampaging rabbits and getting that Ready Brek glow from an old watch

In recent times, one of the big talking points in education has been the gender gap appearing in exam performance. A great deal of research has been carried out into why boys are performing significantly less well than girls, and this has been followed by a plethora of school INSET sessions and working party meetings across the UK. Research has shown that effective use of ICT can have a positive impact on the level of motivation and participation of boys in lessons.

WEBSITE

The Department for Education and Skills Standards website (www.standards.dfes.gov.uk/genderandachievement/) contains a link to a 'raising boys achievement toolkit' which makes several references to effective and 'active' use of ICT having a positive impact on boys' progress.

Boys respond very well to the immediacy of feedback that ICT can give, the fact that you can change a variable easily and immediately see a change taking place. There are a whole range of CD-ROMs and packages available that are attractive to the eye and that contain a high degree of interactivity, that are also well advertised and marketed with a promise of boosting results. It is important, in order to get maximum value in terms of both money and learning impact, that a prospective purchaser thinks very carefully about how they are going to use this software in lessons and how the students will use it. Many of these packages offer a free trial and it is advised that schools make use of this trial period so that teachers can get a clear idea about how they would plan the use of the software into the learning cycle.

Designing an aid package for a hungry world

The following construct activity is best used as part of a lesson on 'healthy diet and the food groups'. In one lesson taught by colleagues, the students entered the classroom to a series of images of starving children in Ethiopia shown on a whiteboard, accompanied by the soulful 'Adagio for Strings' piece of music by Samuel Barber.

People are dying in the world because of famine.....

And we know about it...

The students were then asked to design a practical aid package to send to Ethiopia that would give the starving people all of the food groups that their bodies need. The students were then directed as part of a carousel of activities to spend 20 minutes on the software program, Multimedia Science School Diet Analyser. The students get to choose from an extensive list of foods and as they do so a graph appears showing the amount of grams of each food group.

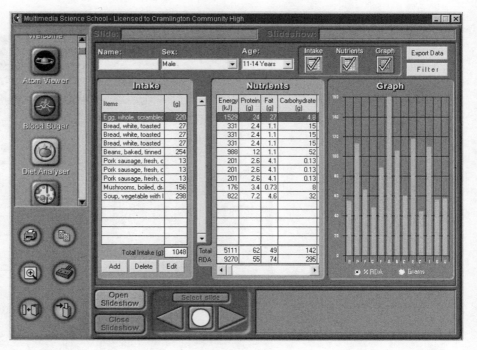

Diet analyser teaching tool

The students can add or delete foods from their chosen lists and experiment until they match the recommended daily allowance criteria that also appear on the graph. The students set about this task with real purpose because of the emotional context of the task and, following their session on the computer, the students were asked, 'What food groups are there?' What food groups are found in cereal – chocolate – fish and so on. To which the students were able to articulate an answer with some confidence.

Multimedia Science School package is a successful and ever evolving CD-ROM package that contains a host of interactive science materials. Here are a few of the activities from the package that really help students to construct new learning.

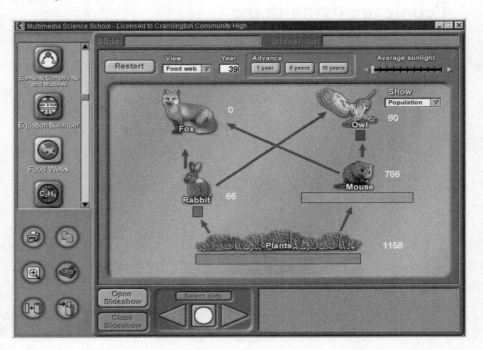

Food webs teaching tool

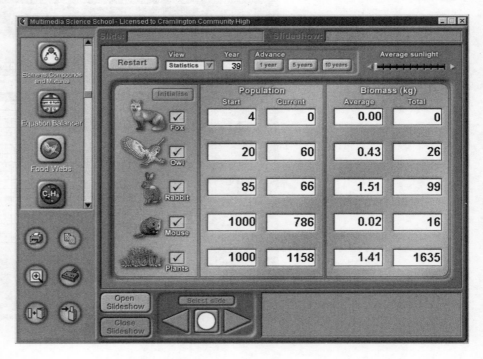

Rampaging rabbits: food webs

In the Multimedia Science School program, students can interact with a food web. Before the students at Cramlington Community High School started using this program, analysis of SAT papers showed that this was an area of weakness in their understanding. The students were demonstrating that when it came to SAT questions that asked, 'What will happen to the number of foxes if the population of owls decreases?' they were unable to apply what they had learned very successfully. This program enables students to change the population of different species and with a quick click to advance the time line. Students can then immediately see what effect this change has had. This is another great example of how the students can play in a virtual laboratory, controling or changing one variable and getting instant feedback on what this change has effected.

The Haber process

In the dreamlike imaginings of the authors, you, the reader, are enjoying this book. You are finding the ideas useful. You are not hating us and are feeling some sort of kinship with us because, after all, we are busy and under pressure teachers, just like you. If you are like-minded souls, you'll be shouting out with joy exclaiming, '*Yessss!, the Haber process! Show me a way to teach this that will not invoke feelings of hatred towards me from the students.*' We shall do our best. This program helps.

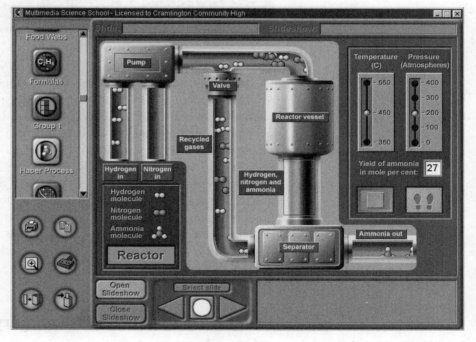

Haber process teaching tool

The Haber process teaching tool of the Multimedia Science School program allows the student to play about with the temperature and pressure of the process and as a result they are given the yield of ammonia produced. By removing the covers of the piping, the students can also see the rate of production of ammonia. In all our years of teaching, this has proven to be the most effective way of getting students to understand the whole pressure/temperature concept around the Haber process: give the students the challenge of finding the best temperature and pressure conditions for the production of ammonia and then simply let them play. They will discover it for themselves.

Radioactive penetration

Radioactive penetration teaching tool

Plutonium and uranium are not the sort of elements that you want your students to get all practical with. Many of the staff in the schools who even keep radioactive sources feel very uncomfortable about carrying out a radioactive penetration demonstration – one teacher we know will only carry out the demonstration with a couple of the thicker lead barriers stuffed down his underpants. With this program (MSS), the students can investigate the penetration of radioactive sources safely such as americium, strontium, cobalt and, rather scarily, an old luminous watch – the kind of thing that you could buy from garages in the 1980s. Turns out, from using the program, that the old watch has the same radioactive count rate as uranium oxide, which is a bit disconcerting to those who wore these watches through their teens. Hope nobody owned a pocket watch version of it.

Using ICT to put scientific enquiry at the heart of science lessons

Many of the activities above help to put scientific enquiry in its rightful place – at the heart of a science lesson. It is surely this, the joy of discovery, of solving mysteries and finding the solution to your own questions, that makes science such a wonderful and exciting subject. It is probably what made you passionate about science in the first place. ICT can help put scientific enquiry at the heart of science lessons – virtual laboratories with their high degree of interactivity can help students to explore, control and discover, offering instant feedback – change a variable and you will see what happens straight away. Irrespective of how good the software package is, however, it cannot beat the thrill of hands on practical investigation. It is what students across the land enjoy the most about the subject of science.

ICT, in particular effective use of data-loggers, can help make practical based enquiry lessons more exciting. Although data-loggers are easy to use and students enjoy using them, it is not the data-logger that makes the lesson more exciting. A data-logger records data, that's all. However enjoyable setting up a practical may be, any experiment that involves any kind of monitoring can be incredibly tedious. All students need to be skilled in reading a thermometer, but who really needs to read a thermometer every 30 seconds? Data-loggers are great for doing the dull things, allowing the students to do something more exciting in the meantime.

Take a cooling curve experiment. As melted paraffin wax freezes, rather than the students religiously recording a thermometer reading every 30 seconds, the experiment can be left running, the real time graph sprouting on the interactive whiteboard or computer screen. During this time, the students can be planning a role play to demonstrate changes of state to the rest of the class – students take on the role of particles in a solid by locking arms together tightly at the elbow to replicate the strong bonds between molecules before they 'melt' by spreading out, only linking by their little fingers to replicate liquid particles. While the role play is developing, other members of the group can be interacting with textbooks or websites to gain a deeper understanding of changes of state and latent heat, in order to make a reasoned prediction about how the graph is going to evolve.

The British government are keen on data-logging. Look at this extract from the QCA programme of study:

ICT statutory requirements
Pupils should be given opportunities to apply and develop their ICT capability through the use of ICT tools to support their learning. Here are the statutory requirements to use ICT in the science programme of study:

Key Stage 1
Sc1 Scientific enquiry
Investigative skills
2g: communicate what happened in a variety of ways, including using ICT (for example, in speech and writing, by drawings, tables, block graphs and pictograms).

Breadth of study
1c: Pupils should be taught the knowledge, skills and understanding through using a range of sources of information and data, including ICT-based sources.

Key Stage 2
Sc1 Scientific enquiry
Investigative skills
2f: make systematic observations and measurements, including the use of ICT for data-logging.

2h: use a wide range of methods, including diagrams, drawings, tables, bar charts, line graphs and ICT, to communicate data in an appropriate and systematic manner.

Breadth of study
1c: Pupils should be taught the knowledge, skills and understanding through using a range of sources of information and data, including ICT-based sources.

Key Stage 3
Sc1 Scientific enquiry
Investigative skills
2g: make observations and measurements, including the use of ICT for data-logging (for example, variables changing over time) to an appropriate degree of precision.

2i: use a wide range of methods, including diagrams, tables, charts, graphs and ICT, to represent and communicate qualitative and quantitative data.

Breadth of study
1d: Pupils should be taught the knowledge, skills and understanding through using a range of sources of information and data, including ICT-based sources.

Key Stage 4 (single science)
Sc1 Scientific enquiry
Investigative skills
2g: make observations and measurements, including the use of ICT for data-logging (for example, to monitor several variables at the same time) to a degree of precision appropriate to the context.

2j: represent and communicate quantitative and qualitative data using diagrams, tables, charts, graphs and ICT.

Breadth of study
1d: Pupils should be taught the knowledge, skills and understanding through using a range of sources of information, including ICT-based sources.

Key Stage 4 (double science)
Sc1 Scientific enquiry
Investigative skills
2g: make observations and measurements, including the use of ICT for data-logging (for example, to monitor several variables at the same time) to a degree of precision appropriate to the context.

2j: represent and communicate quantitative and qualitative data using diagrams, tables, charts, graphs and ICT.

Breadth of study
1d: Pupils should be taught the knowledge, skills and understanding through using a range of sources of information and data, including ICT-based sources.

Data-loggers are for recording data

Sure, data-loggers can be used in clever ways to record data accurately and instantaneously, that is, in real time in the science laboratory or on field trips, data being stored in the memory of the data-logger with a view to connecting it at a later time to a computer (or other hardware) for presentation, analysis and manipulation. Sure, they can speed up experiments, are more accurate and reliable and have real use for recording lengthy experiments, for example, overnight recording. Yes, the data recorded can help to focus on the development of students' scientific enquiry and higher-order thinking skills such as data analysis, interpretation of graphs, result prediction and reflecting on the control of variables. The point is, unless real thought is given about how

CD–ROM Ch3/Resource 7

the data-logger is used as part of the lesson, unless the time the students gain from data-logging is meaningfully used to construct, explore, discuss and think, then there is a danger that the tool can become gimmicky and a bit of an expensive toy. On the CD-ROM you can find a link to download a demonstration copy of LogIT Lab – an easy-to-use data-logging software package for primary schools – together with sample files that can be read and used in the classroom.

Coursework

There are software packages that are genuinely helpful when it comes to collecting evidence for coursework. Focus Educational Software, for example, has produced a step-by-step guide for teachers and students that lead them through the coursework process. There are many suggestions for investigations that might be done in their Science Investigations series, particularly useful for less experienced colleagues and department heads. The software allows you to collect data from the program without the need for any equipment. This would not be a satisfactory situation, but for a preliminary experiment, or for when a student has been absent and needs to catch up, this type of software provides excellent support. It guides the user through the planning, obtaining and analysis stage and even provides a reference section where students can research about the topic.

The screenshots below are examples from **A** the planning stage of an electrolysis investigation, **B** the obtaining evidence stage from a ski jump investigation and **C** the reference section from osmosis.

A

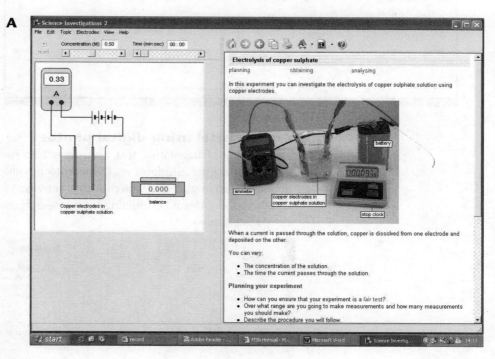

Planning stage

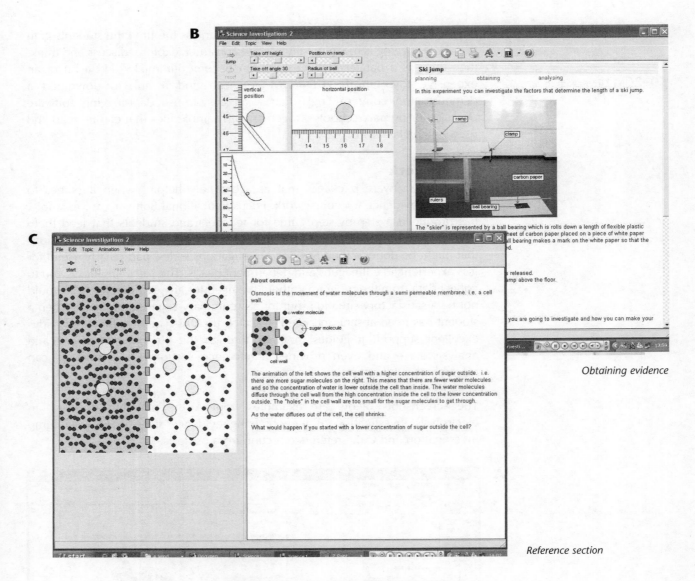

B

C

Obtaining evidence

Reference section

Artist's easel using digital photos

The activity of translating text and ideas into pictures and diagrams can be quite challenging. Students really need to develop an understanding of what they are studying as they attempt this activity. However, it's as useful a tool whether students are conducting their research using online resources or hard copy materials.

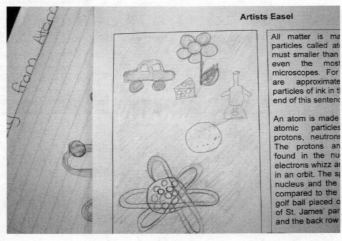

Bringing text to life using drawings

The way in which we interpret learning is unique to everyone

The beauty of this activity is that the pictures students draw are entirely personal. They will make sense to them, but not necessarily to anyone else, including the teacher. As long as they can use the pictures they have drawn as an aid to explain back their understanding to others, then the activity has been successful. Not all of our students will take to this way of learning, but sharing the different types of pictures that other students draw can help to explain why it is a useful tool in their learning kit.

ICT for the boys – use the latest craze

Conversely, the internet is a great place to download free games that could be hijacked and put to educational use, an obvious way to engage our terminally underachieving boys.

I once found myself acquiring a last minute cover lesson towards the end of a long, wet week. *'Happy to help,'* quoth I. On hearing the name of the group my disposition to the news did not improve. My only redemption was that it was a science lesson I was being used for.

With an unamusing and seemingly unamusable group of boys, where containment was often the keyword, I was attempting to get across the niceties of GCSE double award 'work and power'. It would be fair to say that these lads weren't having any of it. Apart from nothing at all, or sending the odd text, all they wanted to do was play the latest free game on the web, which this week was 'smack the pingu' (www.play.vg/games/116-Smack%20the%20Pingu.html). Having been introduced earlier in the week to said website, I could see a deal being struck here.

WEBSITE

Though a ridiculous game – basically you control a yeti with a large club and attempt to 'smack the pingu', the idea being to hit the unsuspecting penguin the greatest distance in the snow – I could see the application to the topic in hand. I gave the class the carrot. If they could deduce the formula for work with me, then I would allow them to smack the pingu and apply the formula to calculate the work done on the penguin. I had their attention. They got straight to the task.

Work done = weight of penguin x distance travelled by penguin

Those who finished working out the formula first were given the task of creating a spreadsheet to record the greatest distance achieved by each student keeping the element of competition alive. Others had to use the internet to research the weight of penguins and agree the weight their penguins should be for the calculations. After each strike, the students used their formula to calculate the work done.

Wanting to cover power in the same lesson we then decided to time the flight of the penguin. This was a task for two people, one to smack the penguin and one to operate the stopwatch (more ICT and collaboration). The whole class were now on task as a competition to find the most powerful club-wielding yeti was underway.

$$\textbf{Power of yeti} = \frac{\textbf{Work done}}{\textbf{Time taken for penguin to land}}$$

The suggestion to set-up a spreadsheet to calculate the power this time came from them, and a couple of students honed GCSE ICT skills at the same time.

Good strike – watch that penguin fly

Final descent

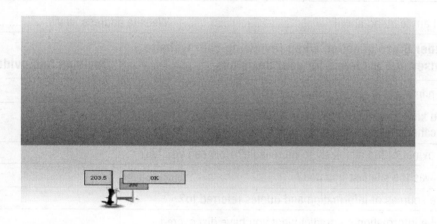

Safe landing – distance travelled 203.5m

Some problems followed (also based around the penguin) that required rearranging the formulae. A review at the end of the lesson, with me having a go at smacking the penguin and a race to calculate sir's power, demonstrated that the majority of the class could correctly manipulate and use the formulas for work and power. Success.

▍ Making sense of the internet

Like many adults, our students tend to think that just because something has appeared on the news, in a book or is on a respectable looking website, it must be true. As we have mentioned already, there is an unbelievable amount of guff on the internet. It is reasonable to expect our students to go online to do research but we must train them specifically to sift the wheat from the chaff. Which of the thousands of websites that are offered when a search for 'food chains' is entered in to a search engine, for example, are likely to be most useful?

Most sites on the internet undergo little or no screening for quality and reliability, certainly far less than a published electronic resource or book and we must ensure our students know this and train them to be critical in their choices of resources. This is more easily said than done but there are resources out there that can help us in this important task. In their publication, Zahava Scherz and Ornit Spector-Levy (1999), suggest a simple proforma for students to fill out as they embark on a piece of research. This prompts them to evaluate the websites they have chosen to look at against certain relevant criteria. They can then compare the reliability and credibility of the information found within them.

The following table has been adapted from *Scientific Communication, Part 1* for use in our school with some Year 10 students, but the language, layout and content will need to be adapted for use in your particular circumstances. We would suggest that re-emphasizing this type of activity regularly throughout a child's education, starting as early as possible and preferably at Key Stage 2, would be most beneficial for them.

Topic I am learning about: .... Website address: www.	
Consider these question when reviewing your website and insert the evidence for your decisions	**Decision and evidence**
Is the name of the editor/author present?	
Do you know their credentials? – Who they work for, qualifications relevant to article?	
Is the owner of the site likely to be reliable? How can you tell?	
When was the site last updated?	
Are the sources of information and quotes referred to?	
Does the information contradict what you have discovered elsewhere?	
Do you think the information that is presented is credible and up to date?	
Is the information helpful, can you use it for your task?	
Is the site easy to navigate? Are there clear headings, a site map, do the links work quickly?	
Does the site use images, animations, video, audio?	
Are the multimedia elements useful or are they gimmicks?	
Is the site attractive or stimulating to use?	

Website evaluation sheet

When time has been spent on a task like this, a simple numerical grade, such as the one on page 73, could then be completed for the website. These grading sheets can then be included on any challenge or activity sheet providing useful information for students starting a similar activity who do not have the time to do a proper review of resources.

CD-ROM Ch3/Resource 8

A digital version of this framework, which you are free to adapt to your needs, can be found on the CD-ROM.

Give marks for the following	1 = very poor 10 = very good
Authority – can we rely on the people who wrote the website?	
Comprehensibility – is the site easy to understand for people in your class?	
Navigation – is it well organized and easy to use?	
Resources – does it have good resources that you found helpful?	
Relevance – did the content of the site match the task you were working on?	
Total/50	

Website grading sheet

This type of activity can be extended to evaluate many resources including newspaper articles, textbooks, magazines, journals and CD-ROMs.

Similarly when creating activities that require students to research and present information from the internet, we must ensure that the potential for cutting and pasting is kept to a minimum. Planning with higher-order thinking activities in mind here can readily eliminate the cut and paste phenomenon.

The subject of audio-visuals and multimedia can also serve as a discussion prompt for the new topic. Obviously this must be used sensibly and sensitively. There is a huge amount of readily available material that you will be able to use with some students in some year groups, but not with others. A good example of this is some of the video footage and commentary that animal rights groups put out. Some of this would be unacceptable to be used with many students, even in Year 11, but would lend itself perfectly to a science for public understanding course, where different points of view, marketing of viewpoints and philosophical issues are considered and discussed.

A more probable reason for caution, though, is caused by the plethora of resources that are available. New resources are being developed all the time, which is a great thing, as there is a need for decent, high quality materials. With many products, however, more time and effort seems to go in to creating the amusing but cute character that appears and waves at you when you get a question right than has gone in to the educational content.

We have all done it, particularly when we first have access to ICT resources, in that we dive in headfirst, especially if it looks good. The resource might initially seem excellent and draw our attention to it. The marketing people do their jobs well. But after some time you discover that you have in fact been wasting your time, with most of the learning happening at a very superficial level. Much of the creative input in to the resource has been focused on the imagery, sound, animations and navigation. What is missing is any worthwhile science. One cannot help but wonder if teachers were even consulted on some of these products. Even some of the more expensive products often fall short when you practise using them. Particularly when you want material for the more able of your students.

Using ICT as interaction-inviting source material

As stated at the beginning of this chapter, ICT has a large part to play in helping students make meaning of often difficult scientific concepts. For the students to make meaning they must be able to receive and/or interact with new information and process this internally, making new connections and applying the new information to other contexts. ICT can provide students with high impact visual source material for them to interact with. Whether the source material is the internet, a CD-ROM, a Camtasia tutorial, a piece of film or television footage, if the students can sit a round a computer screen, either on their own, in a pair or group and spend some time interacting with the material, it can very much support and boost the construction process. Here are some examples that we have seen being used very effectively indeed.

Take a virtual tour

Where do you want to go? The Museo de Jamon in Madrid? A brewery? We have asked students to explore processes and concepts by taking virtual tours on the internet. In one particularly effective example, a class of students were carrying out a project for their GNVQ intermediate science course on a health and fitness module. As part of this assignment, the students had to take on the role of personal trainers to two clients (that is, two of their classmates). The personal trainer had already ascertained their dietary habits from a questionnaire and had put their clients through a series of exercises to gauge their level of fitness and now, in order to meet the success criteria, they had to design a two week fitness regime, personal to each client. The students had to select gym equipment for their clients to use and were finding access to a local fitness centre without subscribing to a £50 a month membership difficult. The teacher provided the students with a hyperlink to a virtual tour of a swanky London gym, which allowed the students to pan around and zoom in on state-of-the-art equipment. While doing so the students had to think about the following questions:

➡ What part of the body is this machine designed to develop?

➡ What is the machine designed to develop – anaerobic or aerobic capacity? Flexibility or power?

➡ How long should the client use this piece of equipment for?

This was a great example of the power of the internet in being able to bring the outside world into the classroom.

Online video

The ICT provision available in schools is evolving and expanding rapidly. ICT equipment that seems technologically advanced and luxurious one year, can become the standard every department has the next. While we promised at the beginning of this book that we would keep in mind that some schools have limited ICT provision, for this book not to quickly become out of date we have had to include some ideas that will soon become ubiquitous in classrooms around the UK. As schools and departments develop their own intranet sites, soon teachers will be making more and more use of streamed video clips from their own digital libraries. This will negate the need for bartering for the television with the lab technician and your colleague in the department (who hogs the television), rolling the television trolley down the corridor, spooling through several 1970s school science programmes in order to show students one relevant ten minute video clip.

The internet contains a feast of online video clips ready for downloading. In recent times we have seen students access video clips of:

➡ hurricanes in a lesson on pressure

➡ CCTV footage from the inside of a supermarket during an earthquake during a plate tectonic lesson

➡ news footage from a Sudan village decimated from the effects of famine for the aid to Africa lesson alluded to on page 61

➡ the 100m final from the world championships, in order for students to calculate the average speed of the athletes

➡ a race between Michael Schumacher's Formula One car and a Euro Jet fighter along an airfield runway

➡ Buzz Aldrin dropping a hammer and feather on the surface of the Moon.

All of these video clips were short and could be easily accessed through intranet links by students during the connection phase or by teachers looking for a highly visual introduction to new learning tool. Most of these video clips came from internet news services like the BBC or CNN, which have a wealth of clips and interactive tutorials which lend themselves to the classroom. The strength of using these sites is that, as much as possible, we need to contextualize the science we teach and the news stories that video clips are connected to put the science in a real world context. A powerful example of this was in a recent science lesson on plate tectonics where the students had to find out about the cause and effects of the Asian tsunami. From the CNN and BBC news websites the students were watching television footage of the tidal wave surging through villages, clicking through a step-by-step animation on the causes of the tsunami and moving their mouse over a map of the affected countries. When the mouse moved onto an affected area, information appeared on the toll of the disaster with further links to interviews and other television bites. Within two news websites, the students had access to everything they needed without having to search through a thousand other websites, many of which would have been far less useful. This further demonstrates that as long as the information is carefully selected the information superhighway that is the internet is without doubt a fantastic resource for students to use.

Online photographs

In the last couple of years, Google, the company behind the internet search engine, have gone absolutely stellar. The Google search engine has become the most widely used among a range of other well established and well advertised companies, and their flotation on the stock exchange has been very successful. In educational terms, the site, in particular its Google image function, is absolutely invaluable, with the site sending its feelers out extensively to provide access to a seemingly inexhaustible supply of images. Alta Vista and Yahoo are just as effective search engines.

Throughout our teaching, using high quality visual images is a central theme – quite right, our sight is the principle sense with which we access the world and ICT can help provide maximum visual stimulation. When we give students new information and ask challenging questions, we should always provide relevant visual stimuli. By showing images to students when you ask them questions, you are freeing up their mental capacities. Listening to descriptions of things that are not present or visible takes mental energy, and by showing quality images, pupils can expend all of their mental energy on considering the question at hand.

How we can use these images to construct

In the following activity, students are given source material with stimulus added. They are then asked to explain what is happening in particular squares on the grid – it could be to describe the energy changes in given grids, or in the musical instrument picture, to describe what generates the sound in a given grid.

Students here are asked to simply put words against the picture to explain what is going on.

Fluorescent light tubes in a field

▌Resources

CD-ROM Ch3/Images A, B
WEBSITE

Odyssey – Matter in Motion

http://www.wavefun.com

This is a molecular simulation program with a difference. There is a large database containing hundreds of molecular models. These use real physical modelling of molecular interactions to show the structures and movements within and between molecules. Interactive activities cover most topics that are studied at higher level chemistry, including thermochemistry, biochemistry, transition metal complexes, acids and bases; and solids, liquids and gases.

CD-ROM Ch3/Resource 9

The user has control over the resource and can rotate, enlarge, zoom in and out of molecules, and choose specific atoms within molecules to focus on or view from. You can also choose the type of display to view the systems you are working on. This resource is aimed mainly at A level chemistry, though it has been used to great effect with GCSE science groups as well. Interactive digital resources are available as well as hard copy sheets that require students to interact with the software. This is one of the best resources we have seen for use at any level in schools. A sample of the software is included as the CD-Rom.

MP3 player with voice recorder

A generic device of potentially great use in the classroom. You can sit among students and record their conversations in a very unobtrusive manner. These can be edited and played back instantly. This is a perfect, and now very cheap, tool for debriefing how well students are working together. There is great benefit from replaying conversations in which students have been discussing science. Ideas can be explored with the rest of the class, particularly as interesting or higher-order thinking may have been occurring. Teachers can also use this device to prepare 'concept audio snippets', a natural progression from the concept cartoon and the concept photo.

CD-ROM Ch3/Image C
WEBSITE

Furry Elephant

http://www.furryelephant.com/content/try/

This is an interactive resource predominantly for use by students to help them come to a better understanding of electricity. Students work through a series of tutorials on aspects of GCSE electricity. Some of the resources are at a very basic level and serve as a revision of Key Stage 3 content. The beauty of this software is that students can work at their own pace and assess themselves as they go along. There are some particularly useful animations on, for example, the difference between AC and DC current. Every page is interactive and conveys information through bright and simple images and straightforward language. Pleasingly, there are no bells and whistles in this product, just sound, well thought out learning.

School science clips – ages 4–11

WEBSITE

http://www.bbc.co.uk/schools/scienceclips/index_flash.shtml

This is a resource aimed at Key Stages 1 and 2 students. Simple diagrams, animations and activities guide students through all areas of primary school schemes of work. This site can be used in conjunction with a set of video resources that the BBC broadcast. The activities are very clearly explained to the students and would be perfect as part of a carousel of activities, each activity taking just a few minutes to complete. They would also be ideal as a whole-class review with the activity being run through an interactive whiteboard.

CD-ROM Ch3/Images I, J, K, L
WEBSITE

Discover petroleum
http://www.schoolscience.co.uk/petroleum/

A multifunctional resource that could be employed effectively from Key Stage 1 right up to GCSE. One game to do with sorting products from oil from other resources helps students to understand just how important oil is to us in terms of its diversity of application. Another game gets students to sort the fractions of crude oil in a refinery according to boiling points. Older students can take a virtual tour of a south coast refinery and look at how and why cracking is an essential part of refining oil.

CD-ROM Ch3/Image M
WEBSITE

Modelling the periodic table: interactive simulation
http://genesismission.jpl.nasa.gov/educate/scimodule/cosmic/table.html

Another high quality resource from the clever chaps at NASA. A common activity done in Key Stage 3 and GCSE chemistry is to take the elements Mendeleev had at his disposal and attempt to form a sensible grouping according to the elements' masses and chemistry. This website makes the exercise interactive and helps students with their ordering by allowing them to check the chemical and physical properties and assign a colour before placing them in the space they think the element should occupy. This is an activity that really brings the history of science to life.

CD-ROM Ch3/Images R, S
WEBSITE

SDBS – spectral database
http://www.aist.go.jp/RIODB/SDBS/cgi-bin/direct_frame_top.cgi?lang=eng

This is a massive database of thousands of organic compounds. It is an excellent resource for teachers looking for resources for their A level chemistry students. You can search the database by number of carbon atoms, empirical formulae, proper chemical or trivial name and a selection of spectra will be offered to choose from. Particularly useful are the high- and low-resolution nuclear magnetic resonance spectra. Also available are mass spectrometer and UV and IR analysis. Really interesting spectral analysis problems can be set using this resource. Great for synoptic problem planning towards the end of A level courses.

CD-ROM Ch3/Image T
WEBSITE

Create your own hurricane
http://www.nationalgeographic.com/forcesofnature/interactive/index.html?section=h

The National Geographic website is a superb resource for many aspects of science. The quality of images and text is perfect for students from Key Stage 3 upwards. In their forces of nature section students can play with conditions to create their own hurricanes, tornadoes, volcanoes and earthquakes.

The hurricanes section contains a useful activity for drawing together lessons on the nature of matter. Find out about the necessary conditions and factors that affect the growth of hurricanes. Particles, density, speed and pressure can all be put into a real and gripping context. Though the link is not direct, some cleverly crafted questions to accompany the activity can relate the science here back to the National Curriculum, if desired. Will they be able to create a force 5 super hurricane or a measly force 1? The challenge is on.

CD–ROM Ch3/Image W
WEBSITE

Jobs in science

http://www.hurricanehunters.com/

This website offers a glimpse into a rather different career choice for people with good qualifications in science. Find out about the day-to-day activities of hurricane scientists. Students can email questions to the scientists, learn how to interpret reports and see just what it is like to fly in to the eye of the storm.

CD–ROM Ch3/Image Z
WEBSITE

Amino acids game

http://www.wiley.com/legacy/college/boyer/0470003790/chapter/chapter_list.htm#chapter_4

A basic 'shoot em up' space invaders game that could be used as a review of the names of the 20 basic amino acids. There is no new educational content in this game but sometimes it is nice to dress learning up as fun, don't you think. The invaders are different amino acids and back at base you have a specific named invader you have to destroy. Points are awarded for the correct one, death if you're wrong.

CD–ROM Ch3/Image BB
WEBSITE

S-cool

http://www.s-cool.co.uk/default.asp

S-cool is a website made for students studying at GCSE and A level. It contains revision sections of essential knowledge as well as interactive revision quizzes. This website is not exhaustive in terms of content but teachers should be able to use some of these resources as reviews and simple demonstrative activities. Students respond very well in general to quiz type questions and S-cool allows the students to take ownership of the answering process, especially if they are given control of the interactive whiteboard. A site worth visiting regularly for review inspiration.

Chapter 4
The demonstration phase

▌Introduction

With Mr Quimby

> *Right then, now that you've learned all about balancing equations, I'd like you to answer questions one to three at the end of the double page spread. Those of you who finish before the bell can try questions four and five as well.*

Bert, who had done these questions while Mr Quimby was wittering on about moles or something, lent you his book for the answers, while he got on with his English homework. You have an understanding with Bert that in return you would help him out in art, as Bert is truly a terrible drawer.

Mr Quimby's lessons were certainly consistent in that during the last 20 minutes you always had to work through the questions at the end of the double page spread you were studying. That way, you were assured, you would be certain to have covered everything in the book. This was a point you could not argue with. Bert had cottoned on to this very quickly and usually had the questions done shortly after the beginning of the lesson (he did all of them as usually the homework was to finish the rest of the questions from the double page spread).

With Mr Hanzo

> *We have discussed the law of 'conservation of mass' and seen how important it is for scientists to be able to balance equations. What I would like you to do now, in your home groups, is to create a short presentation that shows me you understand how to go about balancing different chemical equations.*
>
> *Each home group has a different equation to balance. I would like you to collectively balance your equation and create a short stand-alone presentation that explains to the rest of us exactly how you did it. What processes did you go through to arrive at the answer? By this I mean the*

science and also how you worked together to agree an answer. Everyone should have a chance to contribute. You have 20 minutes to do this. If you find yourself finished early then pick any chemical reaction you have seen during science this year and see if you can create an equation and explain how to balance that too. I expect most groups will have a second reaction completed within the 20 minutes.

Can we do a poster?

Well Bjorn, your group did a poster last time, so I would suggest you produce a slideshow or a short Moviemaker presentation. You can use the digital camera and some plasticine or the molecular modelling kits if you like.

Can we use Moviemaker too?

Bert, I know you are very good with this software, but you used it last time. I'd like all groups to use a different way of presenting this time. Perhaps a poster or a written description. Don't forget we've got the tape recorder, so you could do a spoken presentation, as long as you agree on the script in your group first.

You notice that Mr Hanzo is opening up your class' folder from the school network. He double clicks on a file called 'What makes a great presentation'. Up on the whiteboard is a digital photo of the criteria your class agreed at the beginning of the year as to what makes a good presentation.

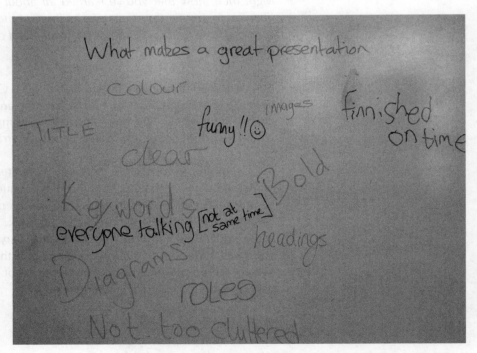

Keeping an electronic copy of previously created classwork allows you to review it whenever you want

Okay, you have 20 minutes. We'll share half our presentations near the end of this lesson and look at the others at the beginning of next lesson, to remind ourselves of how good we are at balancing equations. If there's a spare computer you could use Inspirations to lay out your ideas – remember you can import pictures and add your own notes and audio clips in to this!

▌The demonstration phase

 Another full stop... well death is a full stop... enough of that enough of that... the campus is deserted not surpr... now that's interesting, I've been gazing out of the window for some time but not thinking about what I've been seeing, thinking instead about Isabel Hotchkiss, as if the mind were like a movie camera you can't have a close-up and depth of field at the same time... and as I stopped thinking about her the campus came into focus, or as much as it can this morning with raindrops dribbling down the window panes streaking the dirt, that's the trouble with an all-glass building they badly need cleaning.

David Lodge (2001)

The above is an attempt to record a stream of consciousness, to write down the thoughts that pass through somebody's brain at a given instant. As teachers, we are reasonably skilled at processing these random thoughts in to logically stepped sentences, though when word-processing we will frequently go back over what we have written to amend it.

This linear process of presenting information has its place in schools at all levels and it is necessarily important in preparing our students for written exams. But many of our students struggle with the written word and when asked to apply and demonstrate their understanding in this way they will labour to give quality responses. ICT provides students with a multitude of tools they could use to demonstrate their understanding, text being just one of them.

 You don't really understand something until you can explain it to your *grandmother.*

Albert Einstein

In this section, the learner has the opportunity to apply what they have learned and to demonstrate their new understanding. The teacher may well want to design situations in which students are asked to apply their understanding within a different or unfamiliar context. Certainly this should be about more than simply repeating back information (knowledge is the lowest rung on the ladder in Bloom's taxonomy). The role of the teacher is to provide opportunities for students to explain and apply what they have understood. This may mean, for example, that students present what they have learned to others, and prepare resources for others to learn from.

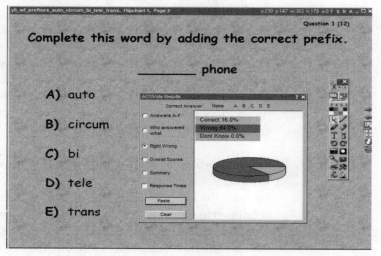

Promethean software showing percentage of right and wrong answers

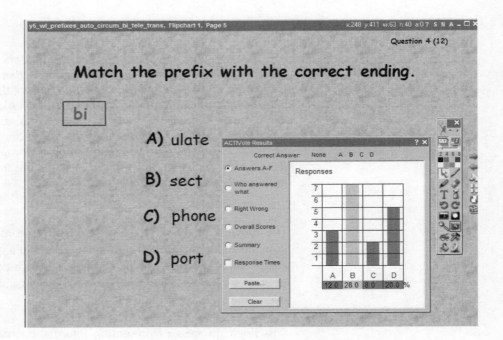

'*Ohhhh, now I get it!*' Don't you just love it when that moment of discovery and understanding washes across your students' faces. Often we strive to explain things in many different ways to get students of all preferred styles of learning to understand scientific concepts. Using the accelerated learning approach, opportunities are built in to every learning experience to allow students to show they really do get it. If they do, then explaining why, to the teacher or to their peers, really helps to embed their understanding. Having to present to their peers ups the ante even further as they don't want to look foolish.

Providing activities where students apply their learning and demonstrate understanding is a key part of the underlying demonstration phase. This chapter suggests some methods where ICT can be employed to create and carry out meaningful and useful activities. Many of these also incorporate aspects of thinking skills and collaborative problem solving.

Voting devices – summative assessment for formative assessment

One GCSE course our students follow is modular and in Year 10 all the exams are multiple choice. Having had experience of filling in the lozenges on the hard copy paper previously, we wanted an assessment that gave feedback quickly and accurately. Students collect their own individually numbered voting device. These can be preregistered (by simply interfacing with a database) so that a particular device corresponds to a particular student. As the students answer their questions the software keeps a record of their answers. This has many benefits, as you can imagine. Perhaps the most joyous is the fact that a class set of 32 scripts does not need to be marked. Reason enough for scraping together a few e-credits.

The real beauty of these voting devices, however, is from an assessment for learning point of view. After each question has been answered the teacher, at a stroke of the interactive whiteboard pen, can analyse the answers students have submitted to the previous question. This may be done for the whole class to see what percentage got the answer correct; or to see the spread of answers (just like in 'ask the audience' from the television show, *Who Wants to be a*

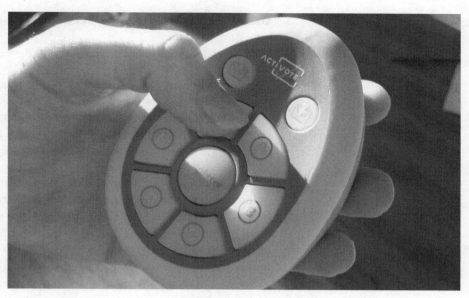

Voting devices are easy for children to use and allow teachers to see the answers entered almost immediately

Millionaire). If the group dynamic permits, students' answers can even be displayed alongside their names.

At the end of the test, you have a comprehensive set of results (that you have not had to mark) with individual and group feedback that can be saved and added to a database for further analysis. By looking at a colour-coded summary of the results, you can instantly see which students have specific problems and which questions the class as a whole found difficult. Doing this type of activity part way through a module or even near the beginning as a form of assessment, gives valuable information to the teacher as to how to modify the next series of lessons. Activities and content can be removed, added and differentiated according to how the students did in the test. You can hear and see the following example in full on the CD-ROM.

CD-ROM Ch4/Resources 10, 11

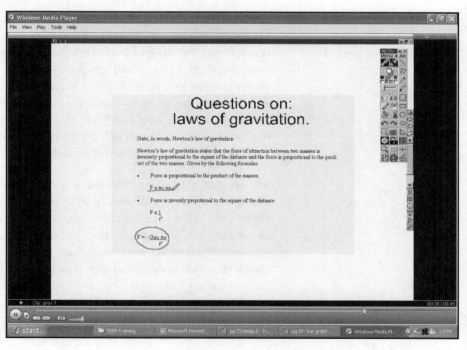

Using Camtasia provides students with useful exam practice

WEBSITE
WEBSITE

Using software such as ScreenFlash or Camtasia

http://unflash.com
http://www.techsmith.com/products/studio/default.asp?lid=CamtasiaStudioHome

These ingenious and readily affordable software programs offer a simple but engaging method for students to record their work. Basically they record all the actions that happen on the screen during any application, including the mouse movements. They can also record sound. They offer students a way to demonstrate their understanding of a topic at their own pace.

Problems answered in this way may often be far superior to the responses given in the classroom. Some students do not flourish when asked to present in front of a class. Removing the stress of direct presentation allows the students to work unimpeded by their reptilian reflexes, urging them to 'fight or flight'. We often expect our students to produce quality responses in a game show time frame, with little recourse to help or consultation. By providing opportunities to use screen capture technology, you also provide them with time to consider and consult various sources before preparing their final answer. Just think what this strategy would allow you to do while on *Who Wants to be a Millionaire*. An answer prepared in this way will, of course, be of much higher quality and the time spent reviewing these answers in class will be of real benefit to all.

Teachers may decide to take the responses in via email, respond to individuals, possibly by adding further verbal commentary themselves and then choose the three or four submissions that stand out to share with the group. This is also preferable to subjecting a whole class to partly cobbled answers. Even the most motivated students would be fading after a few of these. Remember, it is the learning that we should focus on first and then ask how ICT can support us. Using these software applications in this way allows us to monitor and assess, just as we have always done, but perhaps more quickly and in a way more suited to the learning preferences and abilities of more of our students.

Moviemaker

This software comes as standard as part of Windows XP. It allows users to create and edit short movies. Sound can be imported over silent footage and text can be added throughout. The transitions between clips can also be managed. It is quick to get the hang of and simple to use. The clip on the CD-ROM resource was prepared by a small group of Year 9 students to demonstrate their understanding of a specific plate movement (transform boundary, in this case). Researching the boundary and creating the video took just 20 minutes – a length of time we might allocate to a short poster activity. The ease in which real time footage or even still digital photos can be used makes Moviemaker a valid option for short demonstrate activities.

CD-ROM Ch4/Resource 12

We are not suggesting that the students who made this clip know far more about the transform boundary than those who chose to create a poster or a slideshow. What is certain, though, is that they did not copy from a resource, or worse, cut and paste from a website into a PowerPoint slide. They researched using the internet as well as a range of books, had a discussion to check they all understood the concept and then set about *translating* their understanding into *creating* a highly visual presentation. The two words italicized happen to be very higher-order skills according to Bloom's taxonomy. The task appealed to the kinesthetic learners among them. Roles could be assigned to manage resources, tasks and time, and students could work within the group on a variety of tasks. Those who were novice Moviemaker users would also have the opportunity to learn an extra skill on the job.

Children and young people can usually pick up how to use new technology much more quickly than their elders, so it is unreasonable to restrict students to demonstrating their understanding only through mediums which we, as teachers, are familiar with. Many students today are private experts at using software like Publisher, Moviemaker or Photoshop. We may be unfamiliar with these packages but should celebrate the individual skills and competencies that students bring with them. Surely we should be allowing our learners to develop their understanding in ways which appeal to them. A group presentation using a poster that has been worked on collaboratively can be a great way to assess understanding. But a slideshow or short movie, created in the same amount of time, can cover as much information and appeal to many more learning styles and skills. Obviously it is important that these methods of demonstrating understanding are assessed using agreed criteria.

Short movies – video function on digital cameras

Digital video cameras will not be ubiquitous in science departments for a while yet. But the simple digital camera should be. Mobile phones can record audio and video as well as produce quality images of millions of pixels, but digital camera technology is significantly more advanced than this. Two years ago, most camera models offered the facility to record short bursts of moving film at low-resolution. Now even the most affordable digital camera will allow the user to record footage, together with sound, for as long as the memory stick will allow.

So why allow students to record movies when they should be applying and demonstrating their understanding? During certain topics, many science teachers ask their students to demonstrate they understand a concept or an argument by getting them to mock up a conversation between relevant parties, debate an issue or imagine they are tiny particles of rock being weathered, eroded and sent on their merry way through the stages of the rock cycle.

Performing a role play in front of your peers can be a terrifying experience for many of our students. The benefits of recording and playing back your role play rather than performing directly in front of your peers can be manifold. An obvious benefit is that the stress of performing is markedly reduced. The product can be filmed in short bursts, each section being checked for quality and re-shot if necessary, before being combined, rather than having just the one chance to get it right. This gives a greater chance for the science that is being conveyed to be correct. Digital cameras can be connected directly to the display computer and the movie file shared through the projector. A piece of acting displayed in this way also provides greater opportunity for discussion. Specific parts can be revisited at the click at the mouse using the time line bar, whether they are salient points, misconceptions or blatant errors:

This here was a particularly good point, modelled beautifully.

What do you think they meant here?

Can you think of another way they might have done this?

This part here is a common misconception, thank you for pointing it out lads.

Apart from the reducing of stress factor, there is something intrinsically exciting about being on the big screen. Even though some students may cringe a bit at seeing themselves acting, they appear more as part of a team than under the spotlight of a stand-up performance.

Of course, some students will wish to tamper with the footage using software such as Moviemaker, but remember that this method should not take up any more learning time than the non-ICT resourced activity would have taken. A digital video can of course be stored and retrieved conveniently, providing other students with examplar material, revision stimulus and be brought out at parents' evening too! A short clip of a mini-science video would give parents a rare opportunity to appreciate just how enthused, diligent, conscientious, undisciplined or disruptive their cherubs can be.

Big Brother

WEBSITE

Making life easier for the teacher is a great side effect of ICT. Our school has signed up to a revision website – www.samlearning.com. This website allows the students to work through a series of revision exercises and then marks the attempt online, giving instant feedback. The correct answers are not provided immediately allowing the student to go away and revise further before revisiting the exercise.

The beauty of this site is that the class teacher can access the individual students' accounts and see which exercises they have attempted, how they did and how many times they attempted it. Setting these tasks for revision outside lessons has become popular.

'It got wet in my bag.', *'The dog ate it.'*, *'My dad spilled wine on it.'*, will no longer greet you when doing the homework check. Indeed you will know who has and who has not completed the task before the students even arrive at the lesson. Planning for a lesson knowing in advance which students need help, which need extension activities and who has not even attempted the homework/revision exercises is very empowering. It gives you back a great deal of time that is often misspent on non-learning conversations in the classroom.

Getting students to articulate what they were doing at key points in practicals

At Cramlington Community High School, we try and infuse scientific enquiry in to all of our science lessons. Great care is taken therefore, to ensure that practical work is not just being done for the sake of doing practical work and that there is real value in the activity. Many of our colleagues are extremely adept at going around the students during practical work, asking questions that really get the students thinking about what they are doing at key points in the practical. Talking about something as you are doing it, explaining what is happening and why it is happening is a whole brain activity (called pole-bridging).

Another way of making sure that the students are fully engaged with the experimental process is to get the students to articulate what is happening, and why it is happening, by taking digital photographs of their experiment and annotating the pictures using PowerPoint:

Getting students to model scientific concepts

In 1998, I was fortunate to attend a conference in California (in late February when the UK was under a layer of snow – was I popular!), which was all about infusing brain based strategies into the classroom. One of the most memorable sessions I attended was a workshop by Spence Rogers, titled 'Unlocking student's intrinsic motivation'. The workshop was full of practical ideas for enhancing student engagement and one message that came through very clearly related to teaching abstract concepts, something in science we have to do far too often. The core of his message was to 'model it, model it, model it', whether you use role play, plasticine, toys, puppets or footballs for planets, teachers should try and find a way to get the students to bring the abstract concept to life so they can see it and visualize it. Modelling allows children to try out ideas and scenarios that they cannot do easily in real life; and the internet can provide useful activities – see CD-ROM for some examples.

CD-ROM Ch4/Resource 13

When I returned from the conference, highly charged with enthusiasm, I applied the theory as often as appropriate. At this point, I rediscovered a love of plasticine that I had as a child (as a fan of Tony Hart and *Morph*) and resurrected it as a useful learning tool in the classroom. The concept I was trying to get the students to visualize was plate tectonics and the effects that different movement of plates can have for those dwelling on top. The students were given the brief to research plate tectonic movements and to create a slideshow demonstrating the different orientations and effects. The students were then given a digital camera and within 20 minutes of reading and kneading were manipulating the images on PowerPoint slides.

Just because it uses plasticine, it does not mean that this strategy is restricted to use with younger students. I used a similar strategy with A level physics students, who were trying to get to grips with the concept of line defects in material structure and how this can affect the strength of the material. Again, this is a very abstract concept and difficult for the students to visualize, particularly when trying to interact with a very dry textbook. The students used plasticine to create an array of atoms with a line defect and model the effect on the material when shear stress is applied:

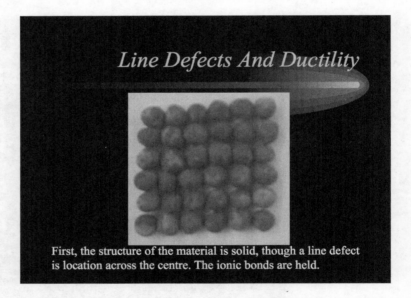

First, the structure of the material is solid, though a line defect is location across the centre. The ionic bonds are held.

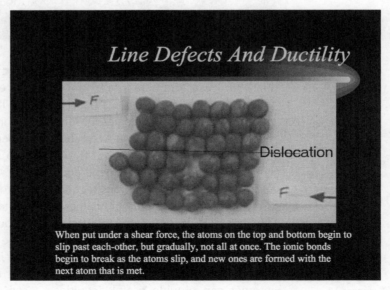

When put under a shear force, the atoms on the top and bottom begin to slip past each-other, but gradually, not all at once. The ionic bonds begin to break as the atoms slip, and new ones are formed with the next atom that is met.

Before the students tackled this activity, I expected them to be less than enamoured with having to use plasticine and a digital camera; however, once the atoms were made, the students began to discuss exactly how the line defect moved through the material.

Useful websites to help students demonstrate their understanding

Go to any of the major internet search engines and type 'Science fun sites' in the search window. The last time I did that the engine returned 129,000 possible websites with that combination of words and, indeed, page after page of search returns promising fun experiments to try at home. Many of these sites were endorsed by parents and it is easy to see the attraction for parents – if their child is going to play games on the internet, make it an 'educational' experience. If you start scrutinizing many of the sites, you will find that the possible relevance to the classroom is somewhat limited.

WEBSITE

There are some exceptions however and one of our favourites for getting students to demonstrate their understanding is www.kineticcity.com. This is a very simple game designed to let students show what they know about the systems in the body. The game puts you in the role of a doctor whose patients' organs have gone missing! Your task is to put the organs back in, system by system as prompted by your assistant. Therefore, when your assistant calls for the respiratory system, you have to drag the appropriate organs across as quickly as possible.

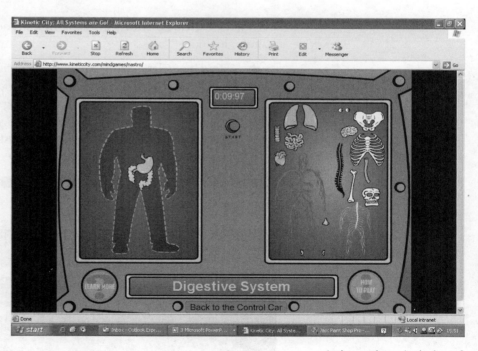

Is there a doctor in the house?

One of the biggest strengths about this site is that it has a number of follow-up activities. First, it puts the student through a debriefing by asking a number of questions:

Did you find out anything you didn't know before?

What do you think would happen if any one of the organs in a system was damaged?

Can you think of other systems in the body?

The questions are designed to get the students thinking about what they have done; an activity which also lends itself to the consolidation phase. The activity then follows up with a less flash, but equally effective multiple choice quiz.

Kineticcity's multiple choice quiz

The other activities, which also follow the 'activity/debrief/multiple choice' pattern, include:

➡ A Touch of Class – a classification exercise
➡ Power Up! – in which your job is to provide power for a gigantic city, without running out of money or ruining the environment
➡ Gravity Launch – in which your challenge is to launch a spaceship from Earth, adjusting the angle and thrust in order to dock the vessel with one or more stations in outer space.

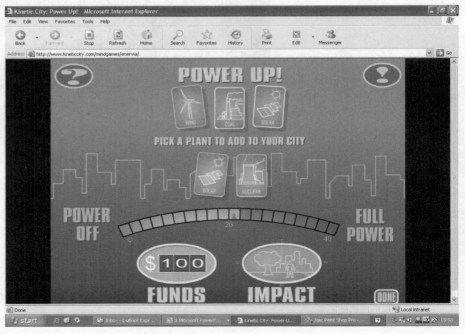

Power Up!

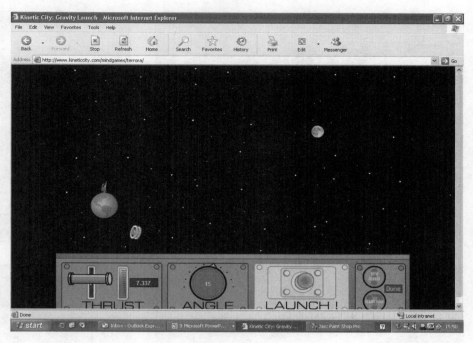

Steady does it!

Bring your toys to life

An activity that appeals to all ages is to convey ideas through making inanimate objects talk. Young children are particularly effective at this anyway. So why not let them be creative in their explanations of scientific phenomenon. One of the most useful resources a teacher can have is a box of junk stashed away in a corner. You would be amazed at how even the most random piece of detritus can be transformed in to an essential bit of kit by a fresh pair of eyes.

Our youngest charges are now familiar with digital cameras and many are mouse-savvy before they get to school. Combining props they are used to, with technology they can grasp very quickly and enjoy using, is a recipe for creativity, fun and collaboration. We have found it takes approximately the same amount of time to train some experienced teachers to use simple PowerPoint functions as it does a Key Stage 1 student.

Whether you give your students a ball of plasticine, a few toys, scissors and glue or ask them to use themselves as the props and characters in the stills, you can expect a range of quality in the products of this type of activity – the same with any activity really. The reason this works particularly well is that it leaves you free to circulate among the groups, asking what they are doing here and there, questioning their understanding of the concepts being studied and differentiating the task by providing targeted support to individuals and groups.

Year 2 students explaining about shadows

Of course, some students may prefer to take their pictures and use them as visual aids while explaining verbally what they understand.

Chapter 5

The consolidation phase

Life without review

Having spent the first half of the lesson trying unsuccessfully to get the digital microscope working through the whiteboard projector, Mr Quimby eventually gave up and directed the class back to their seats.

> *Oh well, not to worry. I think Mr Hanzo must have done something to it last lesson.*

The long delay in starting your own practical of preparing onion cell slides for a normal microscope, meant that everyone was significantly behind as the end of the lesson drew near. There was a sense of anxiety and frustration as some students were unable to follow the instructions on the printed worksheet, while others could not focus the lenses or get enough light through the slides.

The bell for lesson changeover rings. You noticed Mr Quimby looking perplexed and slightly alarmed as members of his next class started arriving at the door.

> *Sir, what do we do with the slides?*
>
> *Put them in the...*
>
> *What about the cover slips?*
>
> *Put the cover slips...*
>
> *I think I've got some onion in my eye!*
>
> *How many times do I have to tell you, don't put...*
>
> *Sir, Lionel just spilled the iodine all over the place and its gone on my shirt!*
>
> *Oh, for goodness sake Roger!*

Amid the mayhem some of your class have started to leave, while the next class have come in and are fiddling with the microscopes that are left on the tables. Bert catches up with you in the corridor.

What was the point of that lesson? he asks.

Not sure really, something about cells and iodine and microscopes I guess. I would have liked to have found out if some other plant cells also look like onion cells though.

Maybe we'll get the microscopes out again next time eh?

Life with review

You can see from the countdown clock on the whiteboard that of the 20 minutes you had for the practical you have just four minutes left. You know that within that time you will have to pack away as well. Mr Hanzo has been visiting each group as the practical was going on, asking question about what you were doing.

Four minutes later: most people have returned to their seats with 15 minutes still to go before the bell. You know that there will be a review of what went on in the lesson, so you have a quick flick through your notes.

While we are waiting for the last group to get back to their seats, spend a moment thinking about one question you would like to ask or something you would like to find out more about. Write it down in the front of your books.

While you do this, you can see Mr Hanzo transferring the pictures he took on his digital camera in to your class folder on the intranet. He was taking photos throughout the practical of each group at work.

When the last group are back in their seats, Mr Hanzo clicks the mouse and a grid appears on the whiteboard. There are four numbers, one for each home group in the class. Mr Hanzo allows the group who finished the experiment to choose first. The Cheeky Monkeys home group plumped for number three. As the cursor rolls over the number their review task, a web quiz, flashes up on the board.

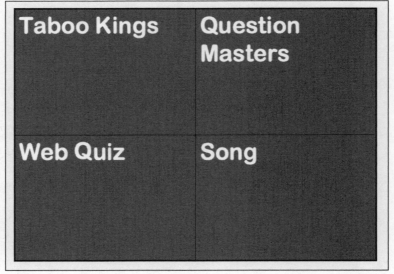

Review tasks

When all of the choices have been revealed, Mr Hanzo briefly explains the tasks.

The Taboo Kings have to create a set of ten taboo cards that can be used next lesson by everyone else in the class. As well as a hard copy version they must also produce a slideshow so that Mr Hanzo can use them with the whole class as a revision exercise before the exams. The Question Masters must go to every member of the class and collect the questions and queries that they wrote down just before the end. These must be collated and condensed onto the minimum number of slides, so that they can be shared with the group next time. These questions will help us to decide the outcomes for next lesson. The Web Quiz people will be using the computers around the lab to revise the content of the lesson online. The web addresses have been taped to the monitors, but you can link to them from today's lesson plan if you like. If you do really well and finish the S-Cool quiz quickly have a go at the level seven quiz on the BBC bitesize website. The Song group has just six minutes to come up with a composition to summarize the main points of this lesson. You will be performing it to the rest of the class at the end. If you want you can choose a tune from the music bank as your backing group.

When all these review activities were completed, and with just one minute left before the bell, Mr Hanzo set the pictures he had taken throughout the lesson to run as a slideshow. You are reminded of the practical you were doing and could see what everyone else was up to as well. One group, you notice, had set-up their apparatus differently from you. That's a good idea, you think and with that you are dismissed calmly. Mr Hanzo at the door bidding each of you goodbye.

The consolidation phase

This is one of the most important stages of the learning cycle and often one of the most overlooked. Too often teachers leave an inadequate amount of time for carrying out a full review, either because teachers are reluctant to interrupt students while they are fully engaged in the activity section or they want to ensure students finish the task. In doing this, the students are missing out on an essential part of the learning experience. As Mike Hughes (1999) describes, learning without regular review is like 'trying to fill the bath without putting the plug in'. Research shows that within 24 hours of a lesson, 80 per cent of content covered is lost, unless it is regularly reviewed within the lesson.

It is during the consolidation phase that students should:

➡ step back and reflect on the learning experience
➡ review the key learning points
➡ be taught memory techniques that will endure and be useful beyond school
➡ reflect on the process of learning (debrief)
➡ preview the next learning steps.

We believe it is extremely important not just to focus on what is learned but how it is learned and we are very explicit about this in lessons with the students. The following are a range of tools and activities to ensure that the students fully reflect on their own learning. Many of these do not require ICT explicitly, but they are enhanced by using it.

The simile

How is the circulatory system like Postman Pat?
How are the food groups like the Bee Gees?
How is radiation like going to the toilet?
How is blood like the army?
How is the solar system like a family gathering (such as Christmas, for example)?
How is a plant cell like McDonalds?

This is a higher-order thinking activity that requires the students to revisit all the learning points of the lesson. Simply display a simile like those above on the whiteboard for the students. As a 'pair/share' activity, ask the students to come up with all the different ways to answer the simile. Ideas can be collated verbally or via a 'Post-it note snowstorm', where students write their ideas on Post-it notes and stick them on the whiteboard. As well as engaging the students, this strategy is designed to help students make the strange familiar and can help give meaning to more abstract concepts. If you can relate the simile to something familiar to the student, for example, Postman Pat, you can use this as a useful 'memory peg' to hook new information on to.

The guided visualization

This comes highly recommended by Alistair Smith who advocates that this should be taught as a technique in primary or first schools. In our experience, we have found this technique to be just as useful right up to A level. The guided visualization will be most successful for those students who are visual learners, and helps get students into a state of relaxed awareness. The visualization can be used to create a sense of awe and wonder or to deliver very abstract ideas (for example, the carbon cycle). The first step is to get the students to relax – use classical or meditation music in the background.

As Alistair Smith (1998) demonstrates:

As you listen to the music, I'd like you to relax. Feel the soles of your feet on the floor, settle down and prepare to enjoy a journey. You may close your eyes if you wish. Breathe deeply. As you listen to the music, relax from the top of your head to the soles of your feet. Enjoy the feeling... (Pause) ... We are about to begin a journey to...

The text should be read with the voice at or just below the level of the music. The language is intended to be suggestive. In other words, you engage the students in asking questions for themselves. This works at an unconscious level, where you are engaging a deep thought structure and not foreclosing on possible answers.

Let students relax in whatever way suits them best

The following technique will have more emphasis if images are being shown on an interactive whiteboard, so that students who do not come naturally to this task, who cannot tap into their 'mind's eye' and create a mind movie, can make mental links much more easily.

Imagine you are a piece of rock on the side of a mighty mountain… (Pause). What do you see, hear, feel? Feel the icy wind chilling the face of the rock… (Pause). Feel the hard rain battering you in wave after wave of icy torment. Feel the rock you are part of breaking up gradually. Suddenly you are washed away by a raindrop, you are part of a very small piece of stone. You tumble down the hill into a small stream which carries you down the hill and in to a big river... You feel yourself being broken and smashed as you tumble along in the river. As you near the sea you become stuck on a sandbank. You are now many grains of sand on the beach. As each day passes, more and more sand is laid on top of you and you become more squeezed. You feel yourself joining onto many other particles until you join into a hard rock... You feel like a complete rock again as you are held together strongly by salts.

You get deeper and deeper underground. It gets hotter, hotter, you feel squashed. You become transformed into a new rock. The heat makes crystals grow around you and you become a beautiful crystal underground. It gets so hot that you feel yourself melting into hot, viscous lava. Big forces send you swirling around deep underground currents near the core. You feel a shake. It becomes lighter, you are so hot everything near you melts instantly, you feel yourself being forced upwards by some gigantic force until BOOM! You are spat out into the atmosphere by a volcano. All you see is smoke and ash and feel the cool air. You settle into a river of lava streaming down a mighty mountain until the river stops. It gets cooler and cooler. You feel more and more solid. Crystals inside you grow and once again you become a rock on the side of a mighty mountain.

Science comic books

'KerPow!' That is the kind of language you would expect to read if you picked up a *Batman*, *Spiderman* or *X-Men* comic, but would it be the kind of sound you would expect to hear from within a science laboratory? Comic books are immensely popular – 10,000 comic books are sold in the UK each day and a number of hit movies and sequels starring comic book characters have dominated recent summer box office charts. Comic books contain lots of science. Pick up any comic book starring *Spiderman*, *X-Men*, *The Hulk*, *The Fantastic Four*, *Superman* or *Iron Man* and you will find throughout the colourful panels and storyline a lot of good science that can be used within the classroom. Some of the science that tends to be thrown at you from a comic book page is often on the fiction side of science fiction, but also within these stories are science questions that ask to be answered:

Where does Bruce Banner's extra mass come from when he changes into *The Hulk*?
What material might his stretchy underpants be made of?
Could Spiderman's web really support a grown man?
How does he stick to walls?
Could Wolverine's cells divide and replicate so fast?

Anyone familiar with comic books can find lots of science in there that can be brought into school and given to the students to interact with, which is always going to go down a storm because of their colourful and fun nature. In one school, the use of comic books has been used in a very exciting way.

Cramlington comics

In February 2004, Cramlington Community High School launched its own comic book company, Cramlington Comics, which produces its own books for use in science and psychology lessons. The idea of using comic books in science lessons came to one of the co-authors of this book (Ken Brechin, the geeky one) one Saturday morning when kicking back to enjoy the latest edition of *Spiderman*, published by Marvel Comics.

On reading the comic and subsequent reading of back issues in the name of research, awareness grew of the science that exists implicitly throughout these particular stories. The thought arose – could we use this in the classroom? Could the science be made more explicit – could abstract concepts be brought to life using comic books? Could we make our own comic books to get across difficult scientific concepts? Are paper based materials the right medium to display these materials? Would the students interact with the comic book storyboard better by using ICT?

At this point, drawing pencils were dusted down and the idea was laid out for a comic book strip starring a new hero, Hadron, doing what new heroes do, that is foiling a bank robbery. The aim of this strip was to get across the concept of Newton's laws of motion, which the students were learning about at the time:

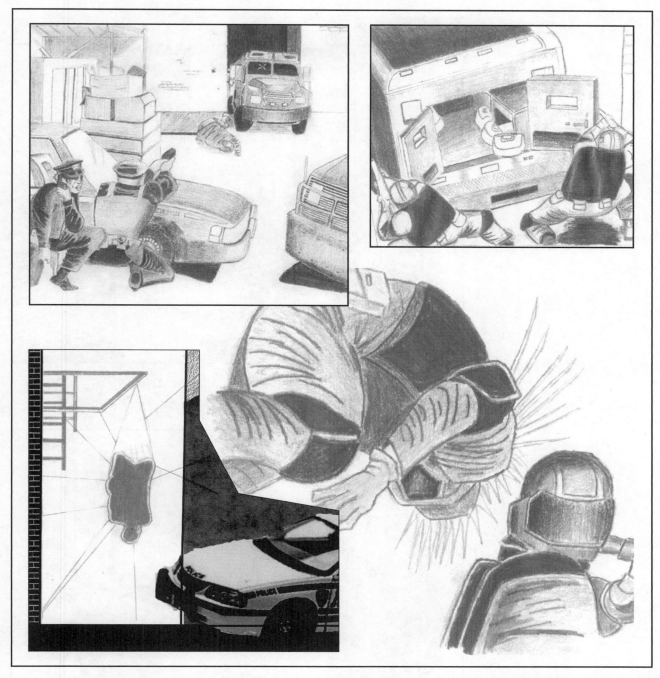

Sketches from Cramlington Comics

To try this out on students, the images were used as a review to the lesson, the pictures were scanned in and displayed on the interactive whiteboard. Instead of just proudly showing the finished story – which would end up as a passive spectator sport for the students – the pictures were jumbled up and given to the students. The task was for them to order the pictures into whichever way they thought would accurately help them tell a story explicitly showing Newton's first, second and third law. Since the pictures had been scanned electronically, the students were able to interact with the pictures online and use PowerPoint and WordArt to generate the text in true comic book style. After 20 minutes, the students were asked to show their storylines to each other – the ease at which their ideas and simple storylines so effectively delivered the science concepts took me aback.

For example:

Physics tells us…

That for every action of force…

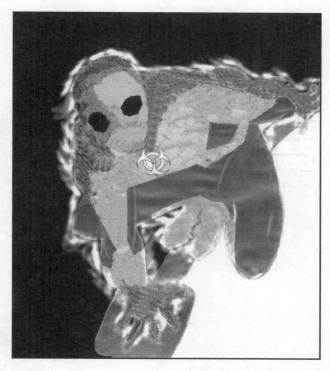

There is always an equal and opposite reaction...

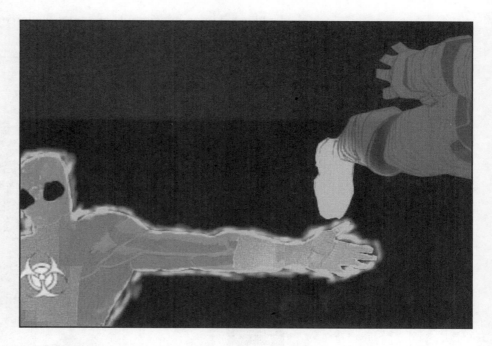

It tells us that a body in motion will remain in motion...

Until acted upon by an equal and opposite force…

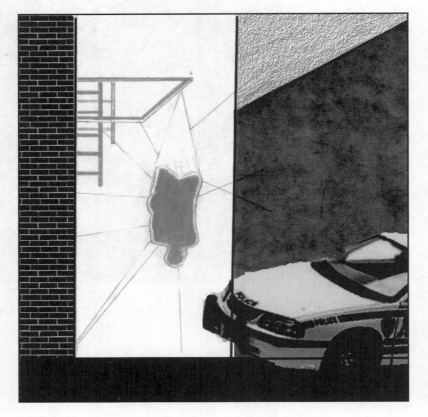

Similarly, an object at rest will remain at rest…

CD-ROM Ch5/Resource 14

The story concluded with Hadron wrapping up the bad guys for the police to take away in true crime fighter fashion. It was at this point that Cramlington Comics was born. An in-house organization generating original science comic book stories created by teachers, drawn by a local pool of talented artists – the students! As well as making a very different, highly effective review activity, this strategy has also been used with great effect to introduce new information, as a central activity or as a way of demonstrating students' understanding. You can find another example on the CD-ROM of how to use a comic book story to engage students with quite difficult science. The PowerPoint resource is yours to adapt to your own needs.

Jan Morton uses comic books to engage students.

Electronic taboo

Everyone knows variations of Taboo – the simplest, of course, and recognized by most students, being *You Say, We Pay* from Channel 4's Richard and Judy chat show. This is one of the most basic games you can play with students with limited resources, as all it requires is keywords on cards. One of its major strengths is that it can quickly reveal the level of understanding of the students, and any misconceptions they have.

To play this, you need a pair of volunteering students, with one of these students in the role of 'guesser', sitting with their back to the whiteboard and facing their partner. The first word should then be revealed. This scientific keyword can be described, drawn, mimed or modelled to the guesser, depending on the level of thinking you wish the students to use.

With a projector and whiteboard you can really up the ante. If you fancy a real challenge, for the students as well as your own classroom management, split the class into two groups. Different members from each group take turns to come up and sit with their back to the whiteboard.

Sperm

Cell	Man
Testes	Whale
Penis	Egg
Sex	Ovum
Reproduction	

Taboo – a great game to get students involved and engaged

In a fixed amount of time, say 30 seconds, the rest of the group has to prompt their team-mate to get the keyword. This activity never fails to bond teams together. It is great fun, promotes teamwork, and if you plan the taboo words carefully, demands high level of thinking and creativity to get the keyword. The key to this activity is to make the descriptions as scientific as possible. Firm rules need to be set. The student saying, '*it sounds like "firm"*' defeats the object as little thinking will occur.

Chillout review

At the end of an all singing, all dancing lesson, full of busyness and student movement, this is the perfect activity to get the students to slow down, calm down, chill out and reflect on their learning during the lesson. Making a chill out review is exceedingly simple – put on some classical or appropriate relaxing music, for example, 'Circle of life' from the *Lion King* for a food chain lesson and let them watch keyword slides go by. Another bonus of doing this activity is that rather than sending the students off to their French lesson high as kites, risking earning themselves and yourself the wrath of the head of modern foreign languages, instead, the students will slope away to French, basking in the calm glory of lots of new science knowledge, permanently stored in their cerebellums. A tutorial describing how to make your own chill out review can be found on the CD-ROM.

CD–ROM Ch5/Resource 15

Songs

I like music in the classroom. I particularly like using cheesy science songs in the classroom, many of which can be found using websites like http://www.acme.com/jef/singing_science/. We have also used a very funny online version of Tom Lehrer's famous elements song which is visually animated and available from http://www.privatehand.com/flash/elements.html. Another way we have used songs is by using the interactive whiteboard to start off a song based on what students have learned that lesson, sung, for example, to the theme tune of *The Flintstones*.

WEBSITE

WEBSITE

In groups, give the students no more than five minutes to think up the words to the song and to sing it out loud to the rest of the class. The students who are musical learners within the class will really love this, as will those who like to perform to a crowd.

This was what one group of students produced from the Alkanes prompt. Genius!

Alkanes, meet the alkanes

They're a hydro-carbon family

Found deep down, under non-porous bedrock

They were formed way back in history

Methane is a great gas for cooking

Naptha makes all sorts like stockings

When you're with the alkanes

Have a long chain sticky tar time

Fly high with kerosine

You'll have an increasing viscous time (as they get longer)

How about this one to the tune of *Roobarb and Custard*? It really helps to play the music to this one, to keep students in time together.

Tectonic plates, tectonic plates,
Move around every day,
Tectonic plates, tectonic plates,
They can make buildings sway,
Himalayas, getting taller,
America moving away,
Convection currents in the mantle,
Swirling around all day.

Tectonic plates, tectonic plates,
Makes the crust move around,
Tectonic plates, tectonic plates,
A jigsaw in the ground!

Keyword Bingo – eyes down!

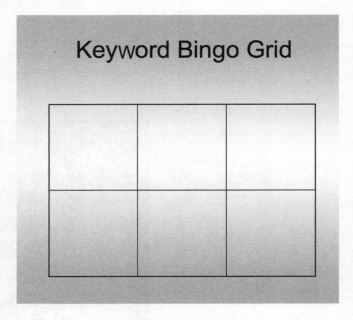

Keyword Bingo
Please select 6 words and place them in your grid.

- Cytoplasm
- Vacuole
- Chlorophyll
- Chloroplast
- Nucleus
- Xylem
- Stem
- Root
- Leaf
- Photosynthesis
- Transpiration
- Root Hair
- Membrane
- Cell Wall
- Carbon Dioxide
- Oxygen

Keyword Bingo Grid

All the materials you need for a game of Bingo!

To play Keyword Bingo we get the students to draw out a simple 3 x 2 grid in their books and to pick six words at random from the list displayed on the interactive whiteboard. The teacher then starts to read out scientific descriptions of the keywords, which the students have to quickly associate to the correct keyword. The teacher can also ask a range of questions, open or closed, to reach out to different types of learner and ability ranges, ensuring there is always challenge in finding the keyword answer. If the students have the correct keyword on their grid, they can cross it off, bingo style. To make the review even more challenging, you can ask the students to choose six numbers at random from a range. Only reveal the words they correspond to after they have chosen. In this way, students will not be able to select words which they perceive are easier, more likely to come up or are more amusing than others.

CD–ROM Ch5/Resources 16, 17

You can find a digital version of Keyword Bingo on the CD-ROM, together with a copy of the bingo grid that you can print out and use with your class.

Pre-SAT review

One recent development in the use of ICT in the science department has been to use PowerPoint review slides as a piece of last minute revision prior to the SATs. How last minute? Well, think of an exam hall full of students sitting at their designated seats, avidly watching a scrolling display of reminders of some of the science concepts they have covered in Key Stage 3, minutes prior to their papers being issued. We trialled this prior to our SAT exams using PowerPoint slides and the feedback we got from the students was positive. Although some of the content did not come up in the exam, students said it helped them to focus and relax into the exam.

Chapter 6

The future or now?

Having been sent by your forward-thinking headteacher to the BETT exhibition to check out ICT innovations and bring back ideas to inspire the science department, you are reunited with Bert after many years. It transpires that both of you, having been to university, travelled a bit and worked in a variety of soulless jobs, retrained as science teachers. You bump into each other at the 'sciBr CaFé' and catch up over a cheekychino. You cannot but help muse over the old days. Both of you remember Mr Hanzo and agree that he had a significant impact on your choice of career.

You are currently a science teacher with responsibilities for ICT, well-being and the woodwind ensemble. Bert also teaches science and is now an assistant year head, logical-consequence co-ordinator and 'science in the community officer'. After gulping down the passable beverage, it's a school day after all, you agree to go and visit Bert at his school next week.

Next week

Bert has just set an assignment. The task is a critical review of a chapter of Bill Bryson's *A Short History of Nearly Everything*. Students are asked to collect their resources. Some head straight for the well-stocked book section and pull down one of the paperbacks. Others are plugging their MP3 players and memory sticks into the computer at the front of the room to download the spoken word version as an audio file. Other students remain in their seats with their mobile phones, Blackberrys, PDAs or laptops and download, via a wireless radio link, the audio and text files of the book. You notice some have already accessed a number of book reviews and are bookmarking the links as favourites.

The criteria for a successful product has been discussed with the class and exemplar material has been peer assessed against the actual mark scheme. Now it is their turn. The students must produce their own individual critical review and, yes, they can choose in what format they submit it.

Oh, I think I'm going to do a podcast from my website this time, says Iqbal.

Fair enough. If you're doing a podcast, drop me an email with the web link when it is complete. Remember, and this applies to all of you, a selection of all the science podcasts from across the school will be uploaded to the school radio website and broadcast at the summer 'Super Science Day'', replies Bert.

If yours is going to be a written assignment, he continues, *avoid giving me paper copies during the draft stage. If you would like feedback as you go along email it to me. I will offer my comments using the editing function and return it to you within a couple of days – do not expect comments on the draft two days before the deadline! Only print out the very final version to go in your files.*

Good idea Bernice. As long as you stick to the deadline and you satisfy all the criteria, you can double up your media studies assignment and produce a television chat show. That could be really good for the 'Super Science Day'. We could have that displayed on one of the big screens in the halls and foyer. Remember to send a copy of your final review to your e-portfolio. This applies to whichever media you've used to present.

Podcasting

A portmanteau of Apple's iPod and broadcasting, podcasting basically allows anyone to make content – usually audio and video, but can include text and images – available for others to download and use whenever they want.

There are significant differences between podcasts and broadcasts. Primarily it is free and legal to podcast, meaning anyone can do it without restriction. Secondly, and more importantly for learners, it is the user, not the broadcaster, who dictates when, where and how the content will be listened to or viewed. The six o'clock news is always broadcast at six o'clock and can be accessed only at six. All major broadcasters archive programmes so they can be accessed by the public afterwards, but they still must be *streamed*, meaning that the user must be connected to the internet the whole time.

Podcasts are essentially all archived from the outset. So it's up to the user when to access them and when, where and how to listen to or view them. Many students, as we know, are not fond of public displays of learning, so learning through their earphones would be a great ruse.

➡ Listen to some French language on the bus on the way home.

➡ History revision in the car on the way over to grandparents.

➡ Catch up with that science video you missed before tea.

➡ Can't read when you're on a coach? – Download the audio version of the set text – you'll have it absorbed in no time.

So they can be used in two ways. Students can create podcasts as a means to present learning. And, as more students get MP3 players and higher specifiication mobile phones, resources can be created at school or downloaded from the internet for students to take home and interact with at their leisure. Schools could sensibly buy class sets for those students without them. Tesco was recently selliong basic MP3 models for £8 apiece – cheaper than the average textbook. This surely is one sea change that students will embrace, as long as teachers can keep up with it.

Videoconferencing

Not a new idea but one rarely seen in schools. The science classroom is ideally placed for videoconferencing bearing in mind the breadth of research and commercial organizations that are keen to be involved in science education at school level. Thanks to voice-over-internet-protocol services such as Skype and cheap and accessible webcams, videoconferencing is becoming as simple as a phone call and is usually now cheaper as long as your school is on broadband.

This is also an excellent way of engendering national and international links and for our students to meet like-minded young people from across the world. Our students will be entering an increasingly diverse workplace, and those who have been interacting and networking beyond their own town will be best placed to succeed. Many of our students never travel beyond a few miles from where they live. Videoconferencing with peers from distant towns and lands would be an exciting and rewarding learning opportunity for any student, of any age.

Conclusion

To reiterate the most important message of this book: regardless of the level of ICT resourcing in your school, the primary focus when thinking about how to apply what resources you have is, 'will this have a positive impact on the learning of our students?'. And this thought should occur only after considering 'what knowledge, skills and dispositions do I want students to develop?'.

As much as possible, we have tried to 'keep it real' with the content of this book, aware that many science departments in schools around the UK may not always have consistent access to computer facilities. If your school is in a situation where many of the ideas discussed here are unworkable, then we would suggest that you are now behind the times. The students we teach are surrounded by ICT, from the moment they wake and throughout the day. Digital radio alarm clocks, video mobile phones, iPods, self-scanning supermarket checkouts, broadband internet access in public telephone booths, electronic tagging. Technology has simply become part of everyday life and as teachers we should embrace, champion and exploit it. Every tool we have discussed is current technology and readily available.

Technology moves at an incredible pace and even two years from now, though many of the ideas and strategies we have suggested will still be valid, there will be a huge number of new resources to help us improve learning. At Cramlington Community High School we have seen our access to ICT evolve over the years, from the solitary departmental computer on a trolley to the present day where we can support all of our lessons with high quality online resources, assisted by our own web design team.

Transferring our teaching and learning resources to an intranet has facilitated the sharing of ideas and has helped to establish consistency in lessons across a large department. High quality lesson planning based on accelerated learning, assessment for learning and higher-order thinking, all supported by effective ICT resources, ensures that our students, whoever they are taught by, get a consistent deal.

We have an ever-expanding arsenal from which to select appropriate tools for learning. When planning lessons, ICT has moved us on from 'I want to get my students to grasp this concept, should I use a card game, graphic organizer, textbook, practical or video?' to 'all of the above plus slideshow, screen capture, interactive mind mapping, animation, internet, voting devices, audio files, green screen activity podcast and more?'.

CD–ROM Ch6/Resources 18, 19

On the CD-ROM you can find an example of how green screen technology can be used. The example contains Mr Brechin explaining Hooke's law in front of some moving animation. This is just one of many interactive resources that will shortly be available to teachers and students of A level physics through the charitable Gatsby Foundation's Teacher Effectiveness Enhancement Programme (TEEP). You can also watch an example of a digital movie put together by teachers. This uses a piece of software called Adobe After Effects to create high quality resources. In the example on the CD-ROM, Mr Brechin spoke into a microphone and gave life to a gas particle.

All of these extra resources have increased the range of tools we have at our fingertips to help unlock students' intrinsic motivation and facilitate learning. We hope this book inspires you to do the same.

References

Becker, H. (2000), 'Pedagogical motivations for pupil computer use that lead to student engagement'. *Educational Technology*, 40 (5), pp.5–17

Betts, S. (2003), 'Does the use of ICT affect quality in learning science at Key Stage 3?', *Studies in Teaching and Learning*, pp.9–17

Bloom, B.S., Engelhart, M.D., Furst, E.J., Hill, W.H. & Krathwohl, D.R. (1956), *Taxonomy of Educational Objectives. The Classification of Educational Goals, Handbook I: Cognitive Domain*. David McKay Company, Inc., New York

Bryson, B. (2003), *A Short History of Nearly Everything*, Broadway Books

Duckworth, J. (2001), *Notschool.net research phase – final report*
http://www.notschool.net/what/pubs/pdf/finalreport.pdf

Gardner, H. (1983), *Frames of Mind: The theory of multiple intelligences*, Basic Books, New York

Harris, S. & Kington, A. (2002), *Innovative classroom practice using ICT in England: the second information technology in education study* (*SITES*)
http://www.nfer.ac.uk/research/down_pub.asp and *Innovative Classroom Practice Using ICT in England: Implications for schools*
http://nfer.ac.uk/research/Downloads/12.PDF

Hughes, M. (1999), *Closing the Learning Gap*, Network Educational Press

Keogh, B. & Naylor, S. (2000), *Concept Cartoons in Science Education*, Millgate House Publishers, Cheshire

La Velle, L.B. et al. (2003), 'Knowledge transformation through ICT in science education: a case study in teacher-driven curriculum development – case study 1', *British Journal of Educational Technology*, 34 (2), pp.183–199

Lodge, D. (2001), *Thinks: A Novel*, Penguin, New York

Mcfarlane, A. & Sakellariou, S. (2002), 'The role of ICT in science education', *Cambridge Journal of Education*, 32 (2), pp.219–232

Osborne, J. & Hennessy, S. (2003), *Literature review in science education and the role of ICT: promise, problems and future directions*, Bristol: NESTA Futurelab
http://nestafuturelab.org/research/review/se01.htm

Owen, W. (1921), *Poems By Wilfred Owen with an Introduction by Siegfried Sassoon*, Chatto and Windus, London

Passey, D. (2000), *Anytime, Anywhere Learning (AAL) Project Evaluation End of First Year Implementation Summary Report*, Lancaster University/AAL

Pedretti, E. & Mayer-Smith, J. (1998), 'Technology, text, and talk: students' perspectives on teaching and learning in a technology-enhanced secondary science classroom', *Science Education*, 82 (5) pp.569–589

Preedy, P. (2002), 'Chris Woodhead meets a headteacher whose progressive ideas have delivered surprising results. For once, jargon that works. We ask pupils to think about what it is like when the teacher is stressed', *The Daily Telegraph*

Reid, M., Burn, A. and Parker. D./BFI (2002), *Evaluation Report of the Becta Digital Video Pilot Project*, Becta

Scherz, Z. & Spector-Levy, O. (1999), *Scientific Communication*, Weizmann Institute of Science

Smith, A. (1998), *Accelerated Learning in Practice: Brain-based Methods for Accelerating Motivation and Achievement*, Network Educational Press

Smith, A. Lovatt, M. & Wise, D. (2003), *Accelerated Learning: A User's Guide*, Network Educational Press

Software and Information Industry Association (2000), *Research report on the effectiveness of technology in schools*, Executive summary
http://www.siia.net/sharedcontent/store/e-edtech-sum00.pdf

Trindade, J. et al (2002), 'Science learning in virtual environments: a descriptive study', *British Journal of Educational Technology*, 33 (4), pp.471–488

Van Daal, V. & Reitsmap, P. (2000), 'Computer-assisted learning to read and spell: results from two pilot studies', *Journal of Research in Reading*, 23 (2), pp.181–193

Acknowledgements

With thanks to the following for permission to reproduce photographs, screenshots, artwork and text in this book and on the accompanying CD-ROM:

Illustrations by Katherine Baxter, pages 13, 35, 99, 106

Richard Box, 'Field' 13.02.04–06.03.04, page 77 (btm)

Brainpop, image Q on CD-ROM

DCP Microdevelopments for LogIT Lab sample files on CD-ROM

DNAI, images D & E on CD-ROM

Focus Educational Software, pages 67, 68 (top)

Furry Elephant 'Electricity Explained', page 60 & images C & GG on CD-ROM

Hurricane Hunters, image W on CD-ROM

Kinetic City images are excerpted from the Kinetic City website (www.kineticcity.com), and are used with permission from the American Association for the Advancement of Science. Copyright 2002-2006, AAAS, pages 91, 92, 93

Leeds University, image AA on CD-ROM

Molecular Expressions, image N, O & P on CD-ROM

NASA/JPL, image M on CD-ROM

National Geographic, images on CD-ROM

National Institute of Advanced Industrial Science and Technology (AIST), images R & S on CD-ROM

Generated with ODYSSEY by Wavefunction, Inc (www.wavefun.com), images A, B & JJ on CD-ROM

All images courtesy of PLATO Learning (UK) Ltd – www.platolearning.co.uk. Images taken from the Plato Learning's Multimedia Science School 11–16 edition, pages 42, 43, 61 (btm), 62, 63, 64

Play VG Games, pages 70, 71

Promethean, pages 83, 84

S-cool, image BB on CD-ROM

Schoolscience, images I, J, K & L on CD-ROM

Softease for sample files created in Textease CT on CD-ROM

The Daily Telegraph, 2002, page 53

'Chapter 1' from Thinks: A Novel. by David Lodge, copyright © 2001 by David Lodge. Used by permission of Viking Penguin, a division of Penguin Group (USA) Inc., page 83

John Wiley & Sons, Inc., image Z on CD-ROM. Screenshot from John Wiley & Sons, Inc.'s World Wide Website. Copyright 2000–2006 John Wiley & Sons, Inc. Reprinted with permission.

With thanks to Tricia Neal, and to the pupils and teachers at Cramlington Community High School for permission to reproduce photographs throughout this book.

Index

cover work 47
Crocodile Clips 59
cross-curricular links 32–3

data-loggers 65–7
Delights of Chemistry 39
demonstration phase 17, 81–94, 109–10
  assessment for learning 84–5
  email 86
  learning styles 87, 109–10
  modelling scientific concepts 89–91
  movies 86–8
  presentations 81–2, 83–4, 86–7
  review 82, 88
  revision 88
  role-play 87
  software 86–7
  toys 93–4
  voting devices 84–5
  websites 91–3
digital cameras
  Artist's easel 68–9
  behaviour management 24–6
  concept photos 56–9
  laboratory safety 26
  modelling concepts 90–1
  planning an investigation 54–5
  practical work 26, 88–9
  for review 26–7
  teasing out misconceptions 56–7
  video function 87–8
Discover petroleum 79
DNAinteractive 38
drag and drop 27–8

Electronic Taboo 105–6
email 86, 110

Focus Educational Software 67–8
food webs 62–3
Furry Elephant 59–60, 78

games 69–71, 80
Google 39–40, 75
graphic organizers 46
green screen technology 112
guided visualization 98–9
Haber process 33, 63
Haworth village 40
homework 88
How stuff works 39
hurricanes 79

ICT
  impact on learning 8–10, 111
  science programme of study 65–6
interactive activities 27–8, 29–30
Internet
  cheat sites 37–8
  evaluation 71–3
  free games 69–71
  in non-networked environment 47
  photographs 75–7
  video files 39, 47, 73, 74–5
  virtual tours 74
  see also websites
intranets 45, 82, 96

Keyword Bingo 108
Kineticcity 91–3

laboratory safety 26
learning environment 12–14, 22–3, 47
learning outcomes 14–16, 34–7
learning styles
  connection phase 32, 33
  activation phase 17, 44, 45, 51–4
  demonstration phase 87, 109–10
  consolidation phase 98
lesson plans 44–5

maths 38
memory 32, 97, 106–7
misconceptions 21, 29, 56–7
missed lessons 45
modelling scientific concepts 79, 89–91
motivation 23, 26, 60, 89
Moviemaker 86–7
  see also digital cameras
MP3 players 110–11
  voice recorders 78
Multimedia Science School 61–4
multiple intelligences 16, 51–4
music and sounds
  for chillout review 106
  for guided visualization 98
  as a memory hook 32, 106–7
  to pick up the pace 31
  to set a calm tone 31
  songs 106–7
  starting a lesson 21, 30–1
  as timing device 31

National Geographic website 78–9

Odyssey – Matter in Motion 78

Network Continuum Education – much more than publishing...

Network Continuum Education Conferences – Invigorate your teaching

Each term NCE runs a wide range of conferences on cutting edge issues in teaching and learning at venues around the UK. The emphasis is always highly practical. Regular presenters include some of our top-selling authors such as Sue Palmer, Mike Hughes and Steve Bowkett. Dates and venues for our current programme of conferences can be found on our website www.networkpress.co.uk.

NCE online Learning Style Analysis – Find out how your students prefer to learn

Discovering what makes your students tick is the key to personalizing learning. NCE's Learning Style Analysis is a 50-question online evaluation that can give an immediate and thorough learning profile for every student in your class. It reveals how, when and where they learn best, whether they are right brain or left brain dominant, analytic or holistic, whether they are strongly auditory, visual, kinesthetic or tactile ... and a great deal more. And for teachers who'd like to take the next step, LSA enables you to create a whole-class profile for precision lesson planning.

Developed by The Creative Learning Company in New Zealand and based on the work of Learning Styles expert Barbara Prashnig, this powerful tool allows you to analyse your own and your students' learning preferences in a more detailed way than any other product we have ever seen. To find out more about Learning Style Analysis or to order profiles visit www.networkpress.co.uk/lsa.

Also available: Teaching Style Analysis and Working Style Analysis.

NCE's Critical Skills Programme – Teach your students skills for lifelong learning

The Critical Skills Programme puts pupils at the heart of learning, by providing the skills required to be successful in school and life. Classrooms are developed into effective learning environments, where pupils work collaboratively and feel safe enough to take 'learning risks'. Pupils have more ownership of their learning across the whole curriculum and are encouraged to develop not only subject knowledge but the fundamental skills of:

- problem solving
- creative thinking
- decision making
- communication
- management
- organization

- leadership
- self-direction
- quality working
- collaboration
- enterprise
- community involvement

"The Critical Skills Programme... energizes students to think in an enterprising way. CSP gets students to think for themselves, solve problems in teams, think outside the box, to work in a structured manner. CSP is the ideal way to forge an enterprising student culture."

Rick Lee, Deputy Director, Barrow Community Learning Partnership

To find out more about CSP training visit the Critical Skills Programme website at www.criticalskills.co.uk